DATE DUE

DEMCO 38-296

58.95
1/14/09

Urban Housing Forms

Jingmin ZHOU

With Introduction by Ian Colquhoun

AMSTERDAM • BOSTON • HEIDELBERG • LONDON • NEW YORK • OXFORD
PARIS • SAN DIEGO • SAN FRANCISCO • SINGAPORE • SYDNEY • TOKYO

Architectural Press is an imprint of Elsevier

Architectural
Press

Architectural Press
An imprint of Elsevier
Linacre House, Jordan Hill, Oxford OX2 8DP
30 Corporate Drive, Burlington, MA 01803

First published in China by China Architecture & Building Press 2001
First published in Great Britain 2005

British Library Cataloguing in Publication Data
A catalogue record for this book is available from the British Library

Library of Congress Cataloguing in Publication Data
A catalogue record for this book is available from the Library of Congress

ISBN   07506 5630 1

For information on all Architectural Press publications
visit our website at www.architecturalpress.com

Printed and bound in China

My heartfelt thanks to all the Architects who provided the material, and to all those people with whom I spoke during visits to the schemes.

Contents

Reason for the Book and Acknowledgments

My childhood and youth were spent in Beijing at a time when the opportunities in China for creative housing design were non-existent. An education in architecture, including a number of research years in Japan and Britain, and latterly in Canada, have opened my eyes to a world of new ideas in housing design. I have been fortunate to travel and see much of this for myself, which has culminated in the production of this book and hopefully two more to follow in the future.

Many of the schemes in the book push out the margins of innovation in response to new housing agendas. Britain and the USA are traditionally more cautious in terms of design than countries in Europe and elsewhere, but a renaissance is now taking place with new design concepts and building forms. My hope is that this book will contribute to this change by bringing together in one publication a range of design ideas from around the world.

I am deeply grateful to Professor Hattori at Chiba University, Japan and Professor Ian Colquhoun of the former University of Lincolnshire and Humberside who introduced me to housing design and gave me initial encouragement to research for this book. Ian has kindly edited the book and written an Introduction. He has also provided information on schemes from the collection he has gathered for his own books. I doubt I could have written this book without this support.

Much of the research was undertaken at Le Soleil Design Studio (Canada), also at University of Montreal (Canada), the University of Lincolnshire & Humberside (now the University of Lincoln), UK, and Chiba University, Japan. My academic colleagues and friends have all provided needed encouragement and support, for which I deeply grateful. My thanks go to Professor Jacqueline C. Vischer, Professor Michel Barcelo and Dr. Charles Cockburn for making research opportunities. Other special acknowledgments are due to Mitsuyuki Aoki, Hajime Yokobori, Suzuki Masayuki and Hiroshi Urushibara, Nakaichi Matsumoto for gathering the material of Japanese schemes; to the Library at the University of Montreal; the Library at Canadian Centre for Architecture (CCA) and the British Architectural Library at the RIBA for the friendly help from the staff. The support of Iwatani Naoji Foundation is much appreciated.

I must express my heartfelt thanks to all the Architects and photographers who provided material, and to all those people with whom I spoke during visits to the schemes. All of them provided me with invaluable insights. The names are too numerous to mention but architects have been credited against their schemes.

I also wish to thank Oliver Irwin for editing in English, Professor Yuan Gao, Amar Baines and Marc Choronzey, and all those who provided language help; also the RIBA (UK), FAB (France), DAL/AA (Denmark), BDA (Germany), BBA (Austria) for helping with visits to schemes. Professor Ian Colquhoun would like to thank Liz Cagney for her secretarial help during the editorial process and the writing of the introduction. I wish also to thank Ian's wife, Christine, whose kindness whilst I was in Britain is much appreciated.

I should like to thank the publishers for all their patience and perseverance; in particular Katherine MacInnes, Alison Yates, Liz Whiting, Catharine Steers (Architectural Press/Elsevier) and Ailing Liu, Fang Xu (Architectural Press of China, who published the book initially in China); also to thank Le Soleil Architectural Press (Canada) for designing and producing the book.

Last but not least I wish to pay particular acknowledgment to my husband, Liyang Sun, and our dear son, Kevin, for their contribution throughout. Liyang took many of the photographs and simply helped with everything. The book would not have been possible without their continual love and support.

Jingmin Zhou
Canada

Introduction: Urban Housing Design

Urban Housing Design

Ian Colquhoun

Introduction

This book brings together many significant grouped housing schemes from around the world. Most are located in cities, are high density in form and illustrate a wide range of design solutions. They are all innovative and many push out the boundaries of experimentation. They share a common theme in being designed with some form of courtyard or green space. This introductory chapter provides an overview of urban housing and analyses the main design criteria for ensuring that it successfully meet the needs of its occupants.

Suburban living in Britain is a reflection of its history and it is still the predominate influence on most people with the means to choose the location and form of their home. In the USA suburbia is part of the American Dream: on a large scale the implications of this kind of density can be seen by the example of Los Angeles where the city spreads over an area half the size of Belgium. There is now a changing climate in both countries as areas of housing policy such as density and design are being openly discussed. In Britain this was stimulated by the publication in 1999 of the report of the Government's Urban Task Force (chaired by Richard Rogers), Towards an Urban Renaissance. [1] In the USA the change of attitude focuses on the New Urbanism movement. The result is that now there is a much stronger commitment to urban living in more compact housing.

The schemes illustrated are all of exceptional quality. However, in looking at those from other countries, it is important to recognise that there are cultural differences to consider. It is all too easy for architects in one country to turn to design models in another without understanding essential social and cultural, and even climatic, differences. Privacy is a high priority for the British: "A truly comparable word for 'privacy' does not exist in French or Italian, yet in England it is one of the country's informing principles". [2] Furthermore, the European model of urban living is different to that of Britain. Historically, apartment living was most common in Europe, whereas in Britain, the pattern was traditionally the house in some form or other with individual accesses at ground floor level.

Occupancy in other countries is also different to that of the UK. In many European countries the emphasis is on customer choice through the rented sector. There is also the difference that people, not homes, are generally subsidised thereby removing the stigma of social housing. Schemes are more often mixed tenure and mixed income and there is more element of choice when people are looking for a home. This frequently results in a much lower turnover of housing occupancy than in Britain.

Overview

Many projects illustrated are strongly influenced by aims and ambitions that go beyond the housing itself - urban regeneration (embracing both new development and refurbishment), experimentation with building form and materials, creating new forms of social grouping, new types of tenure/ occupant, etc. Some schemes are influenced by more than one of these.

Garden City housing
Letchworth

New Urbanist housing
Crawford Square, Pittsburgh
USA
Architects: UDA

London Docklands Housing, Wolfe Crescent
Surrey Quays
Architects: CZWG

Greenland Passage
London Docklands
Architects: Kjaer and Richter of Aarhus, Denmark

Regeneration

London

London and the South East of England are subject to a huge expansion to accommodate unprecedented growth. Much of the new housing has been built in the former docklands covering a total of 8 1/2 square miles. The designs demonstrate a multitude of architectural styles frequently influenced by the developers. One of the most enlightened was Roy Sandhu who commissioned Ian Ritchie Architects to design a small urban scheme - Roy Square - on a derelict site in Limehouse (pp. 209-213). Similarly, in1996 Ballymore Estates commissioned CZWG to design one of the most theatrical schemes in Docklands - Dundee Wharf, which is a significant landmark along the River Thames close to Canary Wharf (pp. 140-144).

Amsterdam

Urban regeneration has been a high priority in the Netherlands for over 20 years also and it is in the new housing developments associated with this that the Dutch have so much to show the rest of the world. The Eastern docklands of Amsterdam have in many places become a magnificent part of the city, heterogeneously designed, modern, and at the same time rooted in the past, matching the spirit and quality of Berlage's Amsterdam Zuid. Plans for the area were approved by the City Council in 1990. The buildings had to be "pleasing and original" and the density high: specifically 100 dwellings per hectare (40/acre). Thirty percent of the dwellings were to be subsidised social housing. [3]

Designs for the new residential areas moved away from large-scale tight physical master plan to a phased approach to smaller scale developments that offer considerable diversity of dwelling types and form. This new approach is particularly reflected in the design of Borneo Sporenburg and the Whale (pp. 244-249).

Berlin

The Internationale Bauausstellung Berlin (IBA) was very significant in the 1980's for rekindling the concept of rebuilding cities within a three-dimensional urban framework established by the nineteenth century pattern of streets, squares, internal courts, parks and public buildings. There was no grand overall plan, nor all-embracing solution. Each urban block, while contributing to the essential realm of the street, was considered to have its own unique spatial quality. Variety was considered essential and individual projects were rarely larger than 150 dwellings. To increase variety, a number of eminent German and international architects were involved in the design of individual schemes. This principle is clearly shown in the scheme on the Fraenkelufer by Hinrich and Inken Baller (pp. 74-77). Herman Hertzberger's housing on Lindenstrasse (pp. 153-157) was also part of an urban block. Local people were invited to join in the planning, and the result was an environment less dominated by architecture and one that left room for the individual.

Paris

During the last 25 years Paris has transformed its abandoned industrial sites with

Successful refurbishment of
1960's high-density housing
Kings Cross, London

Entrepot West Housing
Amsterdam
Architects: Atelier PRO

Piraeus, KNSM Island
Amsterdam
Architects: H Kollhof, CHR Rapp

Berlin IBA Housing
at Fraenkelufer, Kreuzberg
Architects: Inken and Hinrich Baller

new housing and other uses. The vision, promoted by Jacques Chirac whilst Mayor of Paris, was concerned not only with new buildings but with a revaluation of public spaces - streets, boulevards, promenades, squares, riverfronts, parks and the complexities of Haussmann with its city blocks, internal courtyards and passages. The Plan Programme de L'est was a most spectacular instrument to regenerate the whole of the east side of the city, of which the housing schemes in the Bercy Quartier (pp. 222-225) and Rue de Meaux were part (pp. 239-243). The process for designing development areas was to appoint an architect to prepare an overall urban design plan. This stipulated the general composition of the redevelopment - street alignment, massing and heights of buildings, materials, landscaping, etc. This architect would then within this framework coordinate the architects appointed by the individual developers.

The project at the Rue de Balard (pp. 131-134) is part of the regeneration of the site of the former Citroen factory in the south-west of Paris. The core of the project is the Parc de Citroen, which overlooks the River Seine. The axis of the Rue de Balard defines the eastern boundary of the regeneration area and it is flanked on either side by new housing, offices and a hospital.

Small-scale interventions such as the housing development on the Rue de Meaux (pp. 239-243) were just as significant. In their own way they could create a sense of place and be a beacon for the improvement of the whole neighbourhood.

Austria

Few cities can claim to be the source of such challenging designs in housing as Graz in Austria. It is quite remarkable that, within the last 20 years, a city of some 250,000 people has produced at least four architectural practices of confirmed international status and an astonishingly large number of good housing schemes. The Architects were able to experiment with new housing forms and materials to produce designs of exceptional quality because of public confidence in their work.

Japan

The projects from Japan are hugely imaginative. Japanese people have traditionally lived in high density housing in the cities and domestic crime is very low as neighbours respect one another and their property. Density is important in Japanese housing not just because of the shortage of land but extra properties subsidise overall development costs. High-rise super-blocks of 35 storeys or more are impressive and people enjoy the spacious and well fitted out flats and the views. Cars are parked in multi-storey garages or in double layer street spaces.

Orientation is the prime design criterion in Japan to gain maximum benefit from winter sunshine. This results in housing arranged in neat rows set in a landscaped environment. More recently medium rise schemes reflect western designs with housing grouped around more enclosed landscaped pedestrian courtyards as the Kosugi project, (pp. 163-167) and the Theatre of the Ocean (pp. 194-198). The Berlin IBA planning concept of a permeable grid of streets was adopted for the Makuhari "Patios" project at Tokyo Bay (pp. 204-208). It is a very successful and popular scheme with residents but somehow the European model lacks the atmosphere of

Parc Citroën, Paris

New housing
overlooking the Parc Citroen gardens

Early Graz housing
Eisbach Rein, Austria
Architects: Szyskowitz and Kowalski

Housing with good orientation
Tama New Town
Japan

the traditional Japanese city.

Other schemes relate to a deep interest amongst Japanese architects for community architecture, ecological design and sustainable development (Yoga A Flats, pp. 135-139).

China

The pace and scale of change resulting from the urban explosion in China is immense. Everywhere new high-density housing and commercial development is being built. Design follows western architectural styles but a combination of architectural know-how and traditional ideals of "Asian Identity" can produce popular historic themes (Pudong New Area, Shanghai, pp. 189-193).

Many areas of traditional courtyard housing - the Hutong - have been lost in the march of progress. "Hutong" is the northern Chinese term for traditional urban neighbourhoods and it is Beijing's historic form of housing. It is estimated that there are 10 million of this type of dwelling throughout China. Traditionally Beijing was laid out in a rigid pattern with main streets dividing the city into many urban quarters, which were subdivided by a multiple of narrow lanes. Between these lanes, small blocks of high-density courtyard housing developed. Over the years the courtyards of these old brick and timber housing had gradually become infilled with temporary dwellings as pressure on land increased. During the Cultural Revolution the Hutong houses were further sub-divided with whole families accommodated in single rooms. Lack of sunshine and ventilation, drainage and basic sanitation meant that they

became increasingly unwholesome places in which to live. Pressure for development is now threatening this 700-year-old historic urban structure and much has been cleared to provide land for new development frequently in high-rise form. However pioneering schemes such as the Ju'er Hutong Courtyard Housing (pp. 122-125) has helped bring about a reconsideration of planning policies, and the restoration of these historic areas of Beijing. [4]

Design Density

Density and urban housing are inter-linked. Towards an Urban Renaissance, [5] called for liveable urban neighbourhoods designed to higher densities than allowed by planning rules and regulations in Britain - then some 20-30 dwellings per hectare (8-12/acre) (p. 59). The report advised that the most compact and vibrant European city was Barcelona, which has an average density of about 400 dwellings per hectare (162/acre). This compares with typical densities in London as follows. [6]

- Outer suburb - 30 dwellings per hectare (12/acre)
- Inner London housing association scheme - 70 dwellings per hectare (30/acre)
- Victorian Street in Islington - 100 dwellings per hectare (40/acre)
- Street in Kensington and Chelsea - 200 dwellings per hectare (80/acre)

The UK government policy on density is stated in Planning Policy Guidance Note No. 3, Housing (PPG3). Housing developments should be designed to at least 30 or

Left: High quality Japanese housing
at Makuhari

Right: European grid street pattern
Makuhari

Left: Gateway to Hutong courtyard
Beijing

Right: Hutong courtyard, Beijing
China

more dwellings per hectare (12/acre), while 40 (16) is preferred and 50 (20) for urban locations. Higher densities than this are to be encouraged in locations near to good public transport. In London and the South East of England it is clearly recognised that densities need to reflect the twin challenges of housing demand and falling land supply. Density does not affect the image that developers wish to put across in the design of their schemes. A number of schemes illustrated in this book are traditional in approach whilst achieving very acceptable densities (Charles II Place, pp. 109-112, Holyoake Court, pp. 97-99).

However there is a further reason for higher densities. Western Culture has an increasing emphasis on freedom of individual expression, which places new demands on housing. Traditional nuclear families are declining and new household patterns emerging. Couples have fewer children and many more marriages end in divorce, leaving partners on their own or as lone parents. Many young people prefer to live on their own or share accommodation with one or more people. Also people are living much longer lives. These new types of household expect choice and many are deciding to live in the new exclusive high-density developments in town and city centres. High density is clearly on the agenda and quality is paramount.

The essential features for successful high-density development are as follows: [7]

- Accessible location with good transport links to offset the lack of car parking.
- Location regarded as generally "sought after". This can frequently offset desire for lower density housing.

- Generous internal space and storage.
- An adequate infrastructure of shops, schools and other amenities in the area.
- High standards of management and maintenance. Generally as housing density increases, costs in the form of rent and service charges go up too.
- Adequate facilities in the neighbourhood for children.
- Where there are no private gardens some personal outdoor space must be provided, either a well-screened and useable sized balcony (in Britain a conservatory with wide opening windows may be preferable) or a small private garden for a ground floor apartment.
- Comparatively low occupancy level and child densities. A 25% maximum is recommended. Successful schemes have a higher proportion of older residents without children.
- Good security arrangements.
- High standards of finish. The scheme must fit well into the existing urban scale and street pattern.
- High quality building materials that will stand the test of time.
- Good communal facilities, e.g., crèche, elderly people's meeting room.
- External open space and landscaping are crucial to the success of high-density housing.

Two recent publications - by PRP Architects for the East Thames Housing Group Design [8] and Design for Homes/Popular Housing Research [9] - add to this. PRP

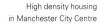
Good courtyard play facilities for children
Olympic Village, Barcelona

High density housing
in Manchester City Centre

Play Area
Slade Green, London

"Une promenade plantee originale"
Rue Malin, Paris

Architects, research of housing development in a number of European countries - France, The Netherlands, Sweden, Denmark - led them to conclude, "the success of high-density housing relates to social attitudes that prevail and the efforts made by landlords and the municipality to reinforce good neighbourly behaviour". It is important for neighbours to be considerate of one another and to cooperate in looking after communal areas. This commitment to good behaviour and good maintenance go hand-in-hand with the provision of good communal facilities by the landlord. [10]

Privacy

In their report, Design for Homes/Popular Housing Research assessed the attitudes of people living in developments in Britain, both private and social, designed to different densities. The overview points to important issues concerning privacy in high-density housing. [11]

- The most important privacy issue is sound transfer between adjoining properties
- Not having sufficient space can present serious problems for occupants. Space is much more important in high-density housing where there is no direct contact with the outside. Rooms must be large enough for their purpose and there must be opportunity for separation of adult from child space. Adequate storage space is essential.
- Privacy in gardens should be ensured with head height walls, fencing and planting so people can relax in privacy.

- Large floor to ceiling windows can be problematic.
- The safety and security of people within their home is a core privacy issue.
- Designing for privacy means designing out crime.
- A degree of community organisation and agreement on shared values was crucial to ensuring household privacy.
- Priorities for ensuring privacy are security, sound insulation, dwelling size, good quality of open space.

Open Space

In his book, A Pattern Language, Christopher Alexander wrote "in order to nourish themselves, people need green open spaces to go to; when they are close by they use them, but if the greens are more than three minutes away the distance overwhelms the need". [12] He defines the term "green" as being "a place large enough so that, at least in the middle of it, you feel you are in touch with nature and away from the hustle and bustle". Both PRP Architects and Design for Homes/Popular Housing Research concluded from their research that some form of open space is vital to the success of high-density housing. Communal open space should give scope for adults to enjoy quiet relaxation and for children to play without causing annoyance to others. The classic "garden square" is preferable located at the front of the properties. This places it more into the public realm than the private, as it would be if located at the rear of the properties. A quiet road, used only for access, creates more distance from the communal open space. If the communal space is at the rear then it is important to

Sibeliusparken, Copenhagen,
good natural
surveillance of
public spaces reduces crime

Starrbacksangen, Stockholm
studied by PRP Architects
Architects: Nyrens Arkitektkontor

Open space formed
within refurbished housing
Kreuzberg, Berlin

Classic London green space
Annettes Crescent, Essex Road
Malmo, Sweden

provide good screening between private gardens and the space. [13]

Good landscaping is important but this must be matched with good maintenance. Public spaces must be clearly defined and overlooked to provide natural surveillance. Play facilities for young children is important where the housing is to accommodate families but there should be provision for older children nearby.

Car parking

Car parking in high-density housing is a huge design problem. Many of the schemes illustrated have underground car parking. In Europe this is made secure with sophisticated entry systems and charges that are acceptable to residents. The best solutions in Britain are those where the planning authority has relaxed standards on condition that residents agree not to have cars (Murray Grove, pp. 217-221).

Community

It is important to create schemes that are not just housing but communities. A most common factor of success amongst the schemes illustrated is the link between privacy of residents supported by a spirit of people coming together. Wherever possible, future residents should participate in the design of the housing. Once occupied the residents should become involved in how the housing is run including its maintenance. This can be achieved through the establishment of residents associations and small management organisations to help regulate and maintain communal open space.

[1] Urban Task Force, Towards an Urban Renaissance, 1999, E and F.H. Spon

[2] Jeremy Paxman, "The English", taken from Design for Homes/Popular Housing Research, Perceptions of Privacy and Density in Housing, 2003, p. 6

[3] Mak. G., and Heddema. F., De Eilanden Het Amsterdam's Oostelijk Havengebeid in Stadsgezichten 1974-2002, English Summary, p. 142

[4] Ju'er Hutong Courtyard Housing Project, Beijing, China, World habitat Awards, Building and Social Housing Foundation, 1993

[5] Urban Task Force, Towards an Urban Renaissance, 1999, E and F.H. Spon, p. 59

[6] PRP Architects, High Density Housing in Europe: Lessons for London, East Thames Housing Group Limited, 2002, p. 13

[7] Colquhoun, I., Design out Crime, Architectural Press/Heinemann, 2004, pp. 102-104

[8] Design for Homes/Popular Housing Research Perceptions of Privacy and Density in Housing, 2003

[9] PRP Architects, p. 7

[10] Ibid, p. 7 [8]

[11] Design for Homes, p. 8

[12] Alexander, C., A Pattern Language, 1977, Oxford University Press

[13] Design for Homes, pp. 12-13

The shop in Homes for Change
helps create community

Creating community
through resident participation

Chapter 1
Density: Under 30 Dwellings Per Acre

Lifestyle in most contemporary cities is rapidly changing and traditional families and extended families are no longer the norm. In line with this social change, Graz in Austria has experienced the conversion into multi-family apartments of many large urban villas on the periphery of the city. They are extremely popular. In this scheme, architects, Szyskowitz-Kowalski have attempted to interpret the theme of urban villas in new development. The site had a slight fall and was of a size to accommodate 4 villas. The design was based on a structural form that allows highly individual and distinct family apartments to be created within a framework of attractive communal spaces. This has resulted in a high degree of social

Credits & data
Location: Haignitzhofweg 7-13, Graz, Austria
Number of dwellings: 14
Site Area: 0.43 ha (1.06 acres)
Density: 33 dwellings/ha (13 dwellings/acre)
Typical dwelling sizes:
    55-140m^2 (592-1,507ft^2)
Number of parking spaces:
    16 underground parking spaces
Structure: Brick, reinforced concrete

Szyszkowitz - Kowalski

Urban Villas Mariagrun

Graz, Austria

1997

1

cohesion within the villas.

The scheme consists of 14 apartments that vary in size from 55-140m^2 (576-1466 sq.ft.). All apartments have their own garden and an unusually large roof terrace. In the centre of the group of villas is a square from which all dwellings are entered via the private gardens. Low walls and a 2-storey high pergola enclose the scheme. In addition there are climbing plants around the square, a row of trees and much greenery.

This challenging design unites the 4 villas into a single comprehensive environment that reflects a new form of community and lifestyle. In addition, the quality of approach has given a small scheme vivid ambience and a memorable architectural image.

Further reading
GA Houses
no. 41, 1994 Mar., pp. 144-152
Text in English & Japanese

2

1   Aerial view
2   Site plan

3

4

3   Path to the square from east
4   View from west, two-storey pergola for climbing plants
    over the square

5

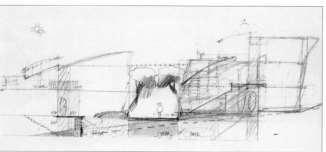

6

7

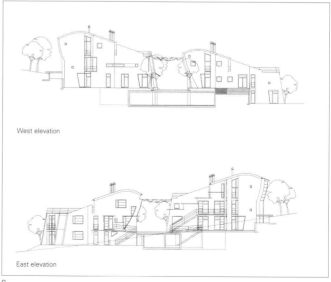

West elevation

East elevation

8

5　View of access
6　Section
7　Façade of the square side
8&9　Elevations
10　Plans

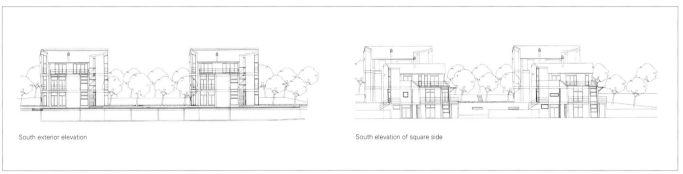

South exterior elevation

South elevation of square side

9

Ground floor plan

2nd floor plan

Underground floor plan

1st floor plan

10

The High Commission (Embassy) in New Delhi contains residential and recreational accommodation together with facilities for administrative and ceremonial functions. Unlike earlier buildings in the High Commission, projects are executed by local architectural practices. In this project Raj Rewal combines a familiar and inviting environment for British born staff with the cultural, environmental and technological factors of traditional Indian architecture. The design combines traditional materials and Indian cluster planning to create a modern, humanly scaled enclave that is skilfully integrated with nature and climate.

The brief called for 12 new three-bedroom dwellings in two sizes. The design is based on low-rise units grouped in four terraces around a central square, all positioned to

Credits & data
Location: British High Commission,
    Chanakyapuri, New Delhi, India
Number of dwellings: 12
Site area: 0.64 ha (1.58 acres)
Density: 19 dwellings/ha (8 dwellings/acre)
Typical dwelling sizes:
    Unit A: 2 no x 222m^2 (2,387ft^2)
    Unit B: 10 no x 191m^2 (2,053ft^2)
Number of parking spaces: 12
Structure: Concrete frame with brick infill wall
    and sandstone cladding externally

Raj Rewal

British High Commission Housing

New Delhi, India
1994

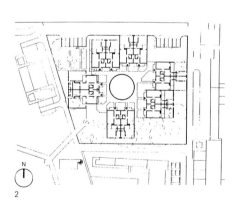

1

respect existing trees and plants around the perimeter of the site. Each dwelling has a private enclosed area at the rear, which reflects the private back gardens of traditional British housing. The ground floor comprises living, dining, kitchen and utility areas and the first floor contains three bedrooms and a terrace. It is the second floor roof of each house, which makes a concession to diplomatic living through its gracious terrace for parties along with roof top umbrellas.

The additional language of the design is based on energy saving devices such as deep set windows, shaded balconies, verandas, roof umbrellas and overhangs, which keep the walls, roofs and windows protected from the sun. The texture of the stone and its changing colour forms an important feature complementing the natural foliage of the site.

Further reading
Architectural Review
vol. 201, no. 1204, 1997 Jun., pp. 58-61
Text in English

Korean Architects
1995 Oct., pp. 58-60
Text in Korean & English

Architecture + Design
vol. 12, no.1, 1995 Jan.-Feb., pp. 54-61
Text in English

2

1   View of Nightingale Courtyard from rooftop
2   Site plan
3   Gateway to Nightingale Courtyard

4

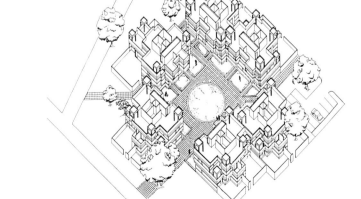

4   View from side entrance
5   Axonometric drawing
6   View of entry from parking

5

6

7

8

Unit A	Ground floor		1st floor

Unit B	Ground floor		1st floor

9

7   View from service entrance (rear courtyard)

8   View of terrace from rooftop umbrella (chattri)

9   Typical plans

Daybreak Grove was commissioned by the North County Housing Foundation, which is a community based non-profit developer. It was financed with a combination of loans and grants from the public and private sectors. It is a housing project for low-income families, particularly single parent, for which the architects made good use of the budget to create a rich design.

The 13 houses are grouped around a central court, which contains shady trees, plots for growing vegetables, a Laundromat and an outdoor theatre. Each dwelling has its own entrance from the street. The sequence of footpath, front garden and front porch continues existing city rhythms and integrates the scheme with the surrounding neighbourhood. Vehicles are allowed access one-way around

Credits & data
Location: 1256 East Washington Ave.,
    Escondido, San Diego, California, USA
Number of dwellings: 13
Site area: 0.34 ha (0.84acre)
Density: 38 dwellings/ha (15 dwellings/acre)
Typical dwelling sizes:
17 no x 2-bedroom dwellings: 67.8m² (730ft²)
6 no x 3-bedroom dwellings: 79.8m² (859ft²)
Number of parking spaces:
    20 (1.5 garage space per dwelling)
Structure: Timber framed

David Killroy Architects

Daybreak Grove

California, USA
1993

1

the perimeter of the site and parking is at the rear of the site so that the main street frontage of entry porches and lawns are not cluttered with cars.

Interior living spaces are organised around a small private courtyard in the tradition of Mediterranean and Latin American quadrangles and its indigenous offspring, the Californian bungalow court. The courtyards provide natural light inside the houses and cross ventilation in every room. The orientation of the kitchen into the courtyard acknowledges its prominence as the focus of family life.

The Residents are involved in daily management and maintenance. As in all successful neighbourhoods everywhere, friendships are made as children play together and adults establish bonds of mutual support.

Further reading
A&U
no. 7(298), 1995 July, pp. 98-109
Text in English & Japanese

Progressive Architecture
vol. 75, no. 5, 1994 May, pp. 49-55
Text in English

Architectural Review
vol. 193, no. 1161, 1993 Nov., pp. 56-57
Text in English

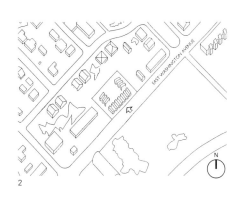

2

1   View on the courtyard
2   Location plan

3

4

5

3   View of stucco planes & curving metal skin roofs
4   Façade from courtyard side
5   Sketch by the architects

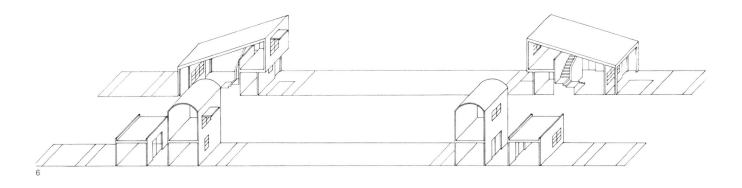

6

7

8

9

6   Isometric section
7   Elevations
      above: Street elevation
      below: Courtyard elevation
8&9   Details of the dwelling

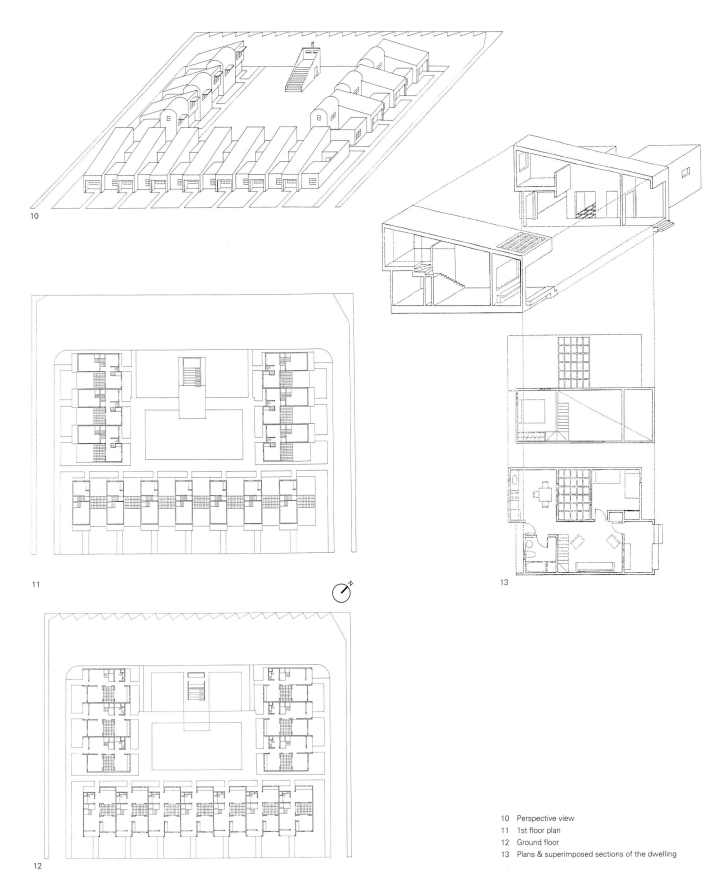

10   Perspective view
11   1st floor plan
12   Ground floor
13   Plans & superimposed sections of the dwelling

Claustro de las Fuentes is built on an urban site and comprises 53 houses, mainly in terraced form. The project's design had two main objectives:

- To create a sense of community
- To ensure a good degree of privacy at high density

The dwellings share common open green spaces designed in a variety of ways to form gardens and plazas. All houses have street frontage and private garden-patios at the rear. A strong sense of community is created through the provision of a multi-purpose recreation area, a children's playground, a community house and swimming pool. Some of the small plazas are covered with "armadas",

Credits & data

Location: Piedras Negras, Coahuila, Mexico
Number of dwellings: 53
Site Area: 1.5 ha (3.7 acres)
Density: 35 dwellings/ha (14 dwellings/acre)
Typical dwelling size: 98m² (1,055ft²)
Structure: Brick, concrete

Mario Schjetnan / José Luis Pérez / GDU

Claustro de las Fuentes Housing

Coahuila, Mexico
1984

1

i.e. timber structures for growing vines, and some have small fountains.

There are two types of two-storey houses. Both are 98m² in area but have different plans. A number of houses are detached and built on individual plots of land within the project.

The construction is load-bearing walls built of hollowed compressed brickwork. The slabs are prefabricated, 300 x 300 x 600 mm in size, set on pre-stressed concrete beams.

Further reading

World Collective Houses: 200 in the 20th century, Yoshinobu Ashihara, Daikyo 30th Anniversary Publication, Japan, 1990, p. 297
Text in Japanese

2

1   View of community spaces
2   Model
3   Ramada: View of convert community plaza

4

4　Children gather around plaza and fountain
5　Internal street: View of houses fronts with garage
　　and service patio
6　Internal Plazas: View of houses
　　and termination pedestrian sequence

5

6

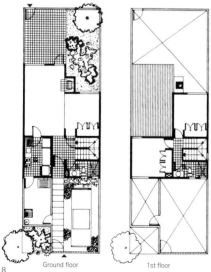

8   Ground floor   1st floor

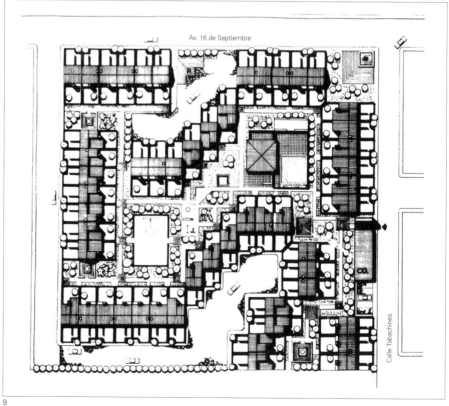

7   View of community houses with swimming pool
     and private courtyard

8   Typical dwelling plans

9   Master plan

9

The Mure housing site is located beside Inokashira Park in a western suburb of Tokyo. Whilst it was meant to convey exclusiveness for high rent investment purposes, its design quintessentially belongs to the traditional Japanese low-cost apartments housing in wooden construction. It is the compilation of this approach surrounding a garden that has made the project financially successful.

The housing is entered through a roofed gate alongside which is a small pavilion used for Boy Scout activities, which the project owner sponsors. Through the gate is car parking and a linear court along which are two blocks of four flats on the north side and three, two-storey houses on the south side. The dwelling plans are conventional with three bedrooms and a "tatami" room (size based on fitting a number

Credits & data

Location: 4-22-16 Mure, Mitaka-city,
    Tokyo, Japan
Number of dwellings: 7
Site area: 0.13 ha (0.132 acres)
Density: 54 dwellings/ha (22 dwellings/acre)
Typical dwelling sizes:
    Flat: 108m^2 (1,161ft^2)
    House: 142m^2 (1,526ft^2)
Number of parking spaces: 7
Structure: Timber construction

Yasumitsu Matsunaga

Mure Housing Project

Mitaka, Japan
1990

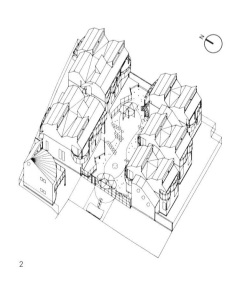

1

of standard sized Japanese reed mats) for guests or elderly people who prefer a traditional life style.

By using the traditional wooden structural system of post and beam, the dwellings have optimum openness to the outside, which is unusual in most modern Japanese housing. In addition the wave-like skylight introduces outside light deep into the interior. Even the bathrooms offer residents a pleasant view of the garden and neighbouring park. This openness is intrinsic in the traditional Japanese concept of residential space.

All dwellings have access by concrete stairs to an island garden seemingly floating in a sea of white sand. The rocks in the garden are from a previous dwelling on the site that was demolished. Bamboo trees have been planted to reduce the cross vision between the dwellings.

Further reading

Housing Developments - New Concepts in Architecture & Design, Kunihiko Hayakawa, Meisei Publications, 1994, pp. 10-16
Text in English & Japanese

Kenchiku Bunka
1990 Jun., vol. 45, no. 524, pp. 165-175
Text in Japanese

Kenchiku Bunka
1991 May., vol. 46, no. 535, p. 97
Text in Japanese

2

1   View of entrance
2   Axonometric drawing

3

3   View of courtyard with gazebo in front
4   Detail of entrance
5   View of courtyard

4

5

6

7

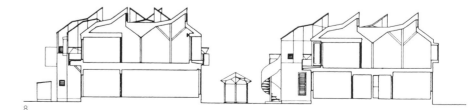

8

6   Night view of courtyard
7   West elevation
8   Section

9

10

11

9   Living room of first floor flat
10 Tatami room looking into courtyard
11 Living room and tatami room
12 Plans

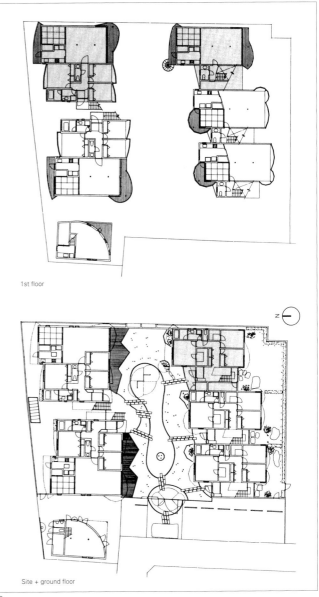

1st floor

Site + ground floor

In all his work, Rolf Keller reflected a dislike of the two principal housing types of contemporary Swiss society, the apartment block and the single-family house. His alternative, as expressed in Chriesmatt, was to create housing more conducive to the growth of a community. The development was financed partly by the architect's family who owned the land, and partly from the pension fund of the food firm, Migros, whose employees bought some of the family house.

The layout centres on a gravel-surfaced pedestrian street running through the site and bordered on either side by flats. Courtyards mingle with the pedestrian street to create a variety of spaces. Access to upper floor dwellings overlooking this street is by means of an external concrete stair and balcony

Credits & data
Location: Chrisematt, Dubendorf,
    Zurich, Switzerland
Number of dwellings: 117
    Dwelling types:
    Flats: 92
Terraced family houses: 25
Site area: 2.5 ha (6.2 acres)
Density: 47 dwellings/ha (19 dwellings/acre)
Typical dwelling sizes: 83-126m^2 (869-1,355ft^2)
Parking: Underground parking

1

Rolf Keller
Housing Chriesmatt
Zurich, Switzerland
1984

2

system with arches beneath providing porches to the entrances of ground floor flats below. The houses curve away at each end of the central street and all have private gardens.

Variety also comes from the use of a large number of dwelling types and through the use of various kinds of windows, oriels, balconies, etc. The design of the exterior is very sculptural. The rugged concrete blocks and slender steel girders stand in sharp contrast with one another, while both join together to show strength. This contrast is applied to many of the architectural elements, e.g. arched porches, balconies, staircases and lamps that regularly appear on the main façades of the flats.

At the north-west end of the site is an ecological pond which took the place of a proposed highway which Rolf Keller success-fully prevented being constructed.

Further reading
Housing Design: An International Perspective
Colquhoun, I., and Fauset, P. G., B. T.
Batsford, 1991, pp. 238-240
Text in English

Architectural Review
vol. 177, no. 1060, 1985 June, pp. 66-75
Text in English

Detail
vol. 24, no. 6, 1984 Nov.-Dec., pp. 675-676
Text in German

Techniques et Architecture
no. 357, 1984 Dec., pp. 115-119
Text in French

1   East façade on the central pedestrian street
2   Site plan
3   View from the entrance hall

4

4   Looking into the pedestrian street from the south
5   Inner small court

5

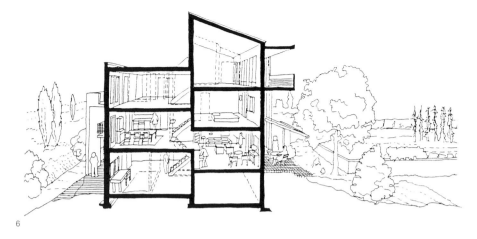

6

6 Section through maisonettes
7 Typical house plans and sections
8 View of the house on the court
9 View of the court

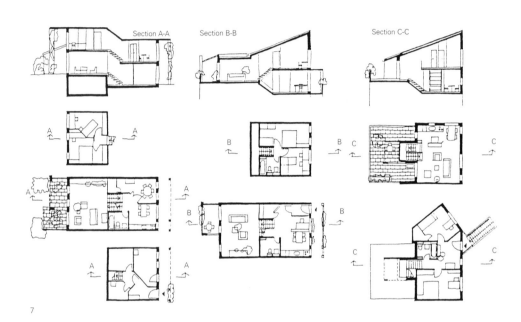

Section A-A   Section B-B   Section C-C

7

8

9

This project is part of Vienna's campaign from the 1980's to update its housing after a long period of inactivity. It was built in the northern outskirts of the city in an area characterised by commercial and industrial buildings and by various types and scales of housing ranging from semi-detached family villas to high-rise courtyard blocks. In such an un-Viennese suburban atmosphere Tsesar's block sits with ease. "It forms an element of measure and summary of its surroundings without claiming to redeem or redescribe the suburb in relation to the glittering magnificence of the city centre. Instead, this unassuming building expresses the inward and calm desire to adapt to what - as a natural and artificial substance - has grown in the course of time in that place." Domus (1986)

The layout draws on the basic vocabulary of

Credits & data

Location: Biberhaufenweg, Vienna, Austria
Number of dwellings: 48
Site area: 0.86 ha (2.13 acres)
Density: 56 dwellings/ha (23 dwellings/acre)
Typical dwelling sizes:
Apartments:
    20 no x 75-90m^2 (806-968ft^2)
Terraced housing:
    28 no x 100-120m^2 (1,075-1,290ft^2)

Heinz Tesar, Otto Hauselmayer, Carl Pruscher

Aspern-Biberhaufenweg

Vienna, Austria
1985

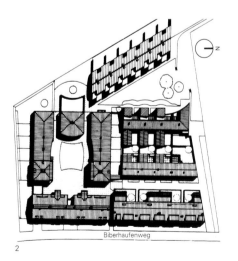

1

urban design: streets, squares and gardens exuberant in greenery. The sensation within the courtyard formed by the inner elevations of its four buildings is of intimacy and calmness. The elevations create a pleasant sense of living in a collective place and of being "enclosed by architecture". The concave and convex surfaces dilate and compress the space and they are marked by the meaningful presence of architectonic features such as thin columns, balustraded stairs, entrances surmounted by triangular tympana and steeply sloping silvery roofs. In this way, Tsesar's courtyard is the "piazza" - the meeting place.

Outside the piazza, the open and mildly urbanised open Viennese countryside is reflected in the external frontages, which are plain and marked by small square and round openings.

Further reading

Bauforum
vol. 18, no. 111, 1985, pp. 51-57
Text in German

Skala
no. 5, 1986 Aug., p. 7
Text in Danish & English

Domus
no. 672, 1986 May, pp. 1-3
Text in Italian & English

2

1   Aerial view
2   Site plan

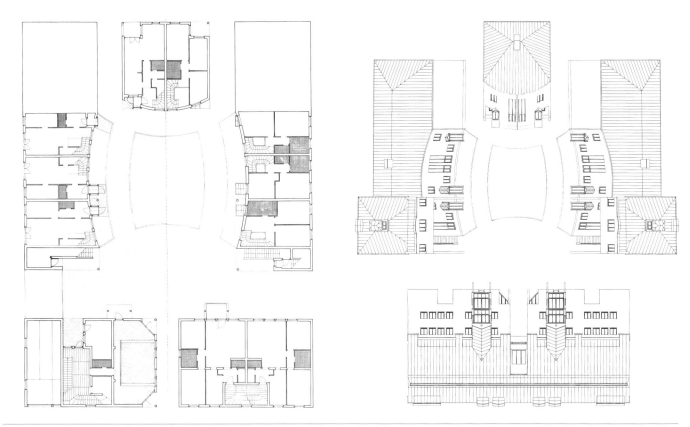

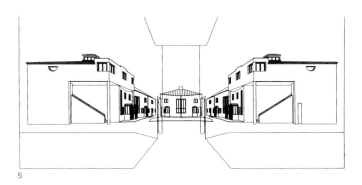

3   View towards the square, A type
4   Plans of A type designed by H. Tesar
5&6 Looking into the square from the entrance, A type

7   Drawings of B type designed by O. Hauselmayer
8   View on the street, B type
9   View of the inner street, B type

8

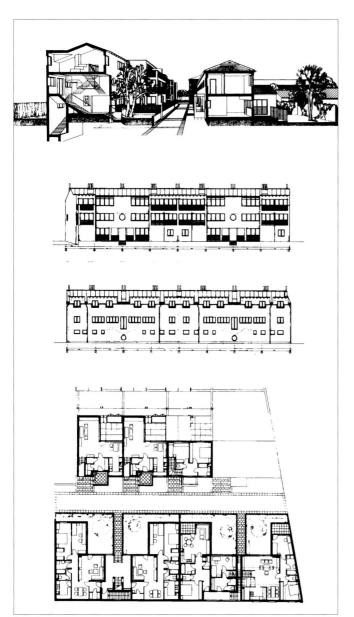

7

9

10

10&11   Exterior views on the courtyard of C type
    12   Drawings of C type designed by C. Pruscha

11

Section of C type

Axonometric drawing of C type

12

This is a most extraordinary project, which looks at issues of design participation, adaptability and flexibility. The scheme takes the form of one long flowing terrace overlooking a peaceful green courtyard that contrasts with the complexity of the building design.

Within the structural system of reinforced concrete frame and load bearing brickwork, every dwelling is custom made according to the requests of the owners. The design also allows for change to be made to individual dwellings. A priority of the architects was that two-level flats should be divisible, allowing adolescent children a degree of independence in so-called "jugenditürme" (youth towers), or even separating off part off the dwelling into a granny flat by adding an independent

Credits & data
Location: 44 Neufeldweg, Graz, Austria
Number of dwellings: 32
Site area: 0.52 ha (1.29 acres)
Density: 62 dwellings/ha (25 dwellings/acre)
Typical dwelling size: 90m² (968ft²)
Number of parking spaces: 32
Structure: Brick construction with reinforced concrete ceiling or reinforced concrete skeleton construction with timber roof structure

Further reading
Housing Design: An International Perspective
Colquhoun, I., and Fauset, P. G., B. T. Batsford, 1991, pp. 220-222
Text in English

Architectural Review
vol. 184, no. 1102, 1988 Dec., pp. 73-75
Text in English

Deutsche Bauzeitschrift
vol. 39, no. 4, 1991 Apr., pp. 495-502
Text in German

Gunther Domenig

Wohnbau Neufeldweg

Graz, Austria
1988

1

entrance. But these opportunities for change and expansion are not the only reason for the loose-fit strategy: the provision of a natural or real structure into which numerous additional elements might be slotted is also important. Balconies and roofs can provide the means for providing extra space, for purposes such as growing flowers or other greenery but could also be used for storage or play by children.

The extensive use of prefabricated concrete planks, aluminium walls and readily available materials for the roofs ensures that the future extensions of the project can be done with ease and economy. Balconies and additional frames for filling-in are on the south side to take advantage of the sun. It is here that lighter fibreboard cladding was used. On the north side there is more corrugated aluminium and brickwork.

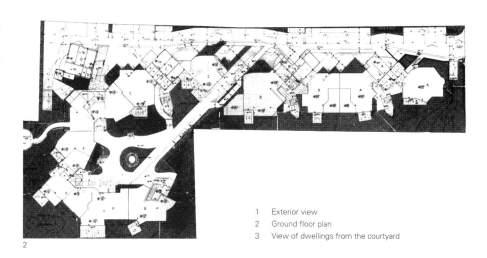

2

1   Exterior view
2   Ground floor plan
3   View of dwellings from the courtyard

3

4

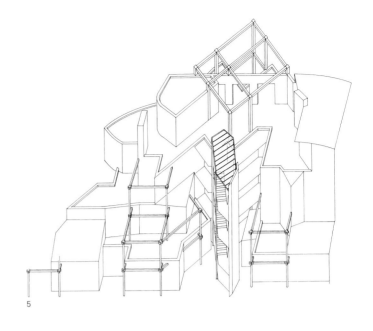

5

6

7

8

4   View of playground
5   Axonometric drawing
6&7 Exterior details
8   Elevations

9   Section
10 Ground floor plan
11 2nd floor plan
12 1st floor plan

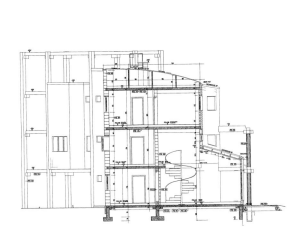

9

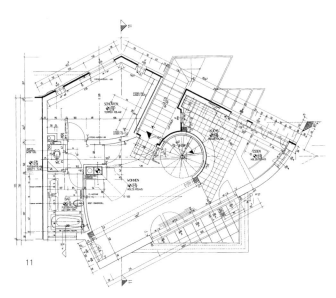

11

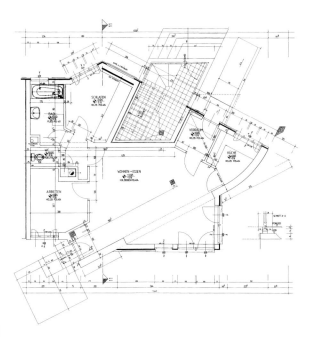

10

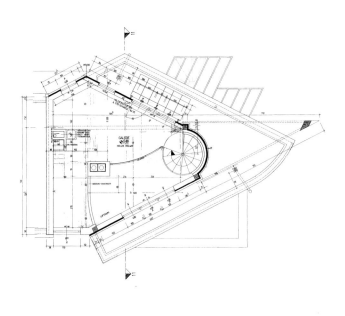

12

In his design Hertzberger has always been concerned with people as well as architectural style. This has been evident throughout all his work in which he aims to create a sense of neighbourliness by exploiting the potential to overlap public and private spaces and create possibilities for multitudes of subtly different uses of space by people (see also his Berlin project (1986), pp. 153-157).

The site of the project at Duren is in a dreary part of the town. Hertzberger took up the challenge of bringing fresh life to the area by designing a square block of housing around a spacious courtyard, which clearly belongs to residents only. The courtyard contains playgrounds and space for community activities that can be watched from all around, as can the children who play there. All entrances to

Credits & data
Location: Rotterdamer Strausse,
    Duren, Germany
Number of dwellings: 136
Site area: 2.5ha (6.18 acres)
Density: 54 dwelling/ha (22 dwellings/acre)

Herman Hertzberger

Housing in Duren

Duren, Germany
1997

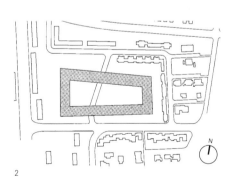

1

dwellings are from the courtyard and upper floor dwellings are reached directly by stairs or over various galleries.

Beyond this, the traditional city perimeter block was turned inside out. Hertzberger retained a public road through the site to maintain the link between the development and its surroundings. Furthermore he located private gardens on the outer side of the perimeter block thereby turning streets into gardens and the internal courtyard into an enclosed city square.

In the façade design, the appropriate scales and the various openings develop the Hertzberger style of harmonisation. This is especially true of the continuous roof, which unifies the whole complex and also acts as a shelter, or an umbrella to ensure the residents are not prohibited from communal activity in wet weather.

Further reading
Industria Delle Costruzioni
vol. 32, no. 321-322, 1998 July-Aug., pp. 4-11
Text in Italian & English

Domus
no. 803, 1998 Apr., pp. 18-25
Text in Italian & English

de Architect
1998 Mar., pp. 72-77
Text in Dutch. Summaries in English

Casabella
vol. 60, no. 630-631, 1996 Jan.-Feb., pp. 72-85
Text in Italian & English

2

1   View of A type building facing the courtyard
2   Site plan
3   View of C type building facing the street

4

5

4   View of B type building facing the courtyard
5   Terrace of C type building

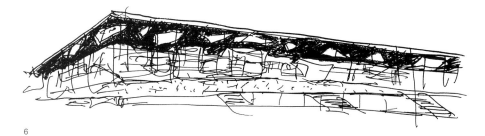

6 Study sketch
7 Sections A, B, C type
8 Typical plans of A, B, C type
9 Ground floor plan

6

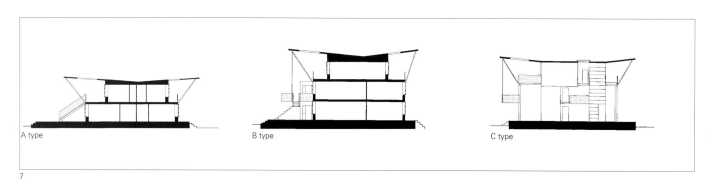

A type   B type   C type

7

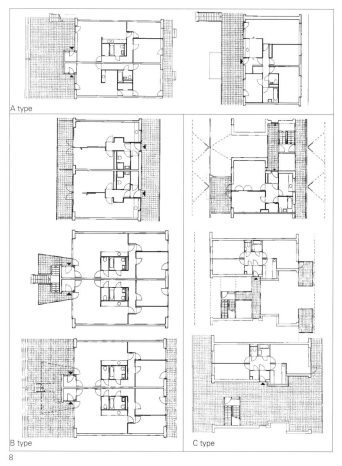

A type

B type   C type

8

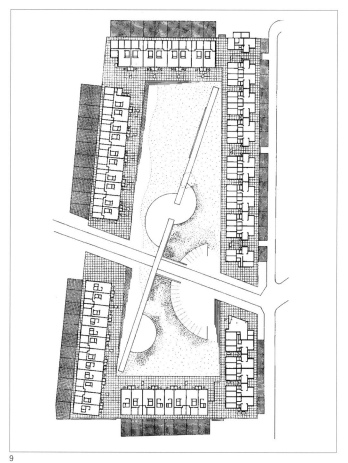

9

Graz has a highly distinguished record for its modern housing design and Karla Kowalski and Michael Szyszkowitz are amongst the most inventive architects. "Their work is organic in the best sense: highly honed to human use and need; the resulting internal spaces are carefully articulated on the outside" (AR 11/99, p. 47). Their scheme at Schiessstatte illustrates these principles very well.

The plan for the whole hillside site with its signature curving internal pathway, originated with architect Heiner Hiezegger who was commissioned by a housing co-operative to create the basic overall plan. He invited several architects from Austria and other countries to design parts of the scheme. The most remarkable feature of the Szyszkowitz-Kowalski portion is the slightly curved long row of

Credits & data
Whole Site
Location: Nordberggasse 44, Graze, Austria
Number of dwellings: 250
Site area: 4.1 ha (1.7 acres)
Density: 61 dwellings/ha (25 dwellings/acre)

Szyszkowitz-Kowalski phase
Number of dwellings: 35
Typical dwelling sizes:
Maisonettes: 90m² (968ft²)
Flats: 50m² (538ft²)
Number of parking spaces:
45 open parking spaces
Structure: Brick, reinforced concrete

Szyszkowitz-Kowalski
Schiessstatte Housing Complex
Graz, Austria
1999

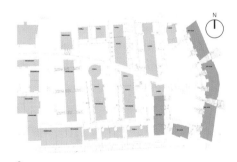

1

buildings, which is formed from paired two-storey maisonettes on the side wings with flats in a three-storey block in the middle section. These are reached directly up glazed open stairs from the public footpath. Each dwelling is given a sense of place and outdoor territory by careful manipulation of plan and section, whilst interiors, though partly standardised, vary in accordance with household size, orientation and view. All dwellings have large private balconies or roof top terraces. Car parking, served by a distributor along the south side of the development, is built into the hill under the dwellings so that the front, west facing gardens of the maisonettes are half a storey above the public green.

In these ways, the design carefully combines both social diversity and a sense of community.

Further reading
Architectural Review
vol. 206, no. 1233, 1999 Nov., pp. 47-51
Text in English

New Apartment Buildings (Architectural Design)
Arian Mostaedi, Leading International
Publishing Group, 2003
Text in English

2

1   Aerial view
2   Site plan of whole complex

3

3 View on the courtyard
4 Exterior view of courtyard side
5 Elevation
6 Section

4

5

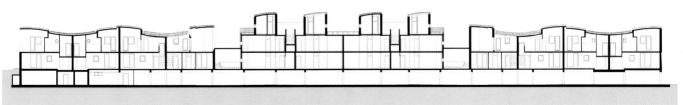

6

7

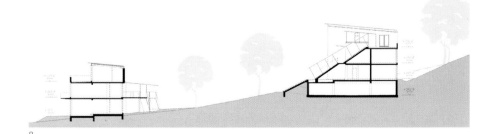

7   View of access stairs
8   Cross section

8

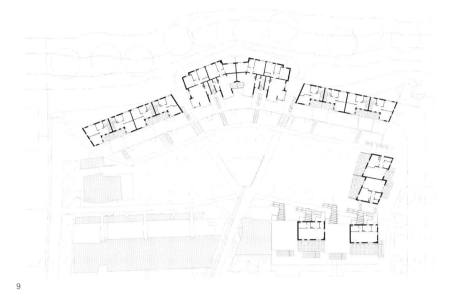

9

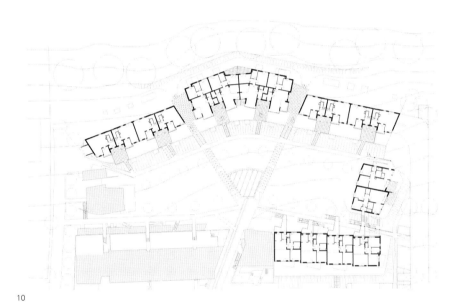

10

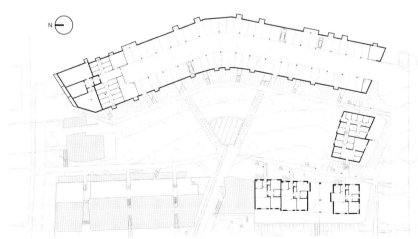

11

9 2nd floor plan
10 1st floor plan
11 Ground floor plan

Inken and Hinrich Baller are noted for the richness, variety and originality of their work which blends building technique with technical innovation whilst opinions of the potential customers is a very important part of the process.

The Fraenkelufer is a part of the Kreuzberg district of Berlin that survived the Second World War almost intact. In the 1960's and 1970's it was proposed to redevelop the site with high-rise housing so the interior of the site was cleared. Whilst the housing on the perimeter, along the Landwehrkanal was preserved, it too was beginning to be destroyed. Under the aegis of the Internationale Bauausstellung Berlin (IBA) the Ballers decided to save and improve the housing frontage along the canal and make two gap sites into gateways entering

Credits & data
Location: Luisestadt, Kreuzberg,
　　Berlin, Germany
Total number of dwellings: 88
Courtyard dwellings: 48
Gate building: 40
Site area: 1.29ha (3.19 acres)
Density: 68 dwellings/ha (28 dwellings/acre)
Typical dwelling sizes:
　　2-bedroom flats: 55m^2 (591ft^2)
　　3-bedroom flats: 80m^2 (860ft^2)
　　6-bedroom maisonettes: 166m^2 (1,785ft^2)

Inken & Hinrich Baller

Housing on Fraenkelufer

Berlin, Germany
1984

1

into a garden court. The existing buildings were restored and alongside the back of the court, a new single aspect building was created which runs up against the firewall of an adjoining industrial building.

The scale of the new development admirably matches the existing buildings. Windows and entrances of the dwellings all face into the courtyard, which is very softly planted and very artistically paved. The Ballers' confidence that their sweeping balconies, when covered in trellises and plants, would help blend old and new, was richly rewarded. A third infill piece turns the corner of Fraenelufer and Admiralstrasse, thereby completing the composition. The scheme is quite unique and a lot was achieved within the tight cost constraints of IBA's social housing programme.

Further reading
Architectural Review
vol. 176, no. 1051, 1984 Sept., pp. 30-34
Text in English

GA Houses
no. 23, 1988 Aug., pp. 136-143
Text in English & Japanese

A&U
no. 12(195), 1986 Dec., pp. 75-130
Text in English & Japanese

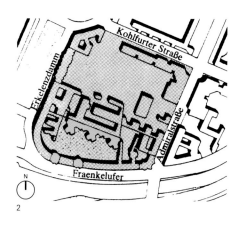

2

1　Exterior view
2　Location plan

3

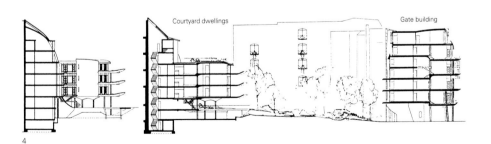

Courtyard dwellings   Gate building

4

3   Façade
4   Sections

5

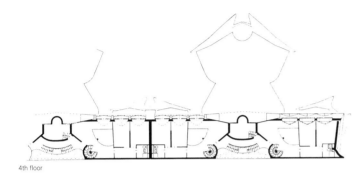

4th floor

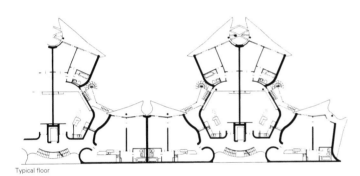

Typical floor

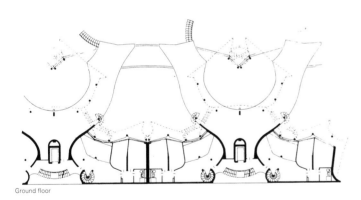

Ground floor

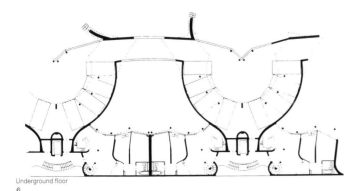

Underground floor

6

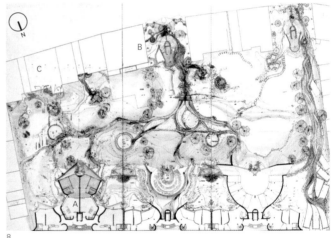

7

8

5   View of the courtyard
6   Floor plan of block A
7   Detail
8   Site plan

This development of 634 dwellings is the first two of seven phases of a rental housing project that will eventually comprise a total of 2,100 units. It provides a unique and timely solution to contemporary high-density urban rental housing for young professional workers in the Californian Silicone Valley who find themselves renting for longer due to the high cost of buying their first home. It admirably meets their demand for higher quality housing through creating a leisure atmosphere with amenities that include a clubhouse, pools, aerobics classes, concierge service, maid service, etc. The ambiance is present in every aspect of the design through the Mediterranean Village character in the layout, the colouring of materials and detailed design. In this way the design evokes a distinct lifestyle and

Credits & data

Location: 1500 Vista Club Circle, Santa Clara,
   California, USA
Number of dwellings: 634
Site area: 9.2 ha (22.7 acres)
Density: 68.9 dwellings/ha (27.9 dwellings/acre)
Typical dwelling size: 47-118m^2 (509-1,270ft^2)
Number of parking spaces:
   1,141 (1.8 space/dwelling)
Structure:
   Wood-frame / Wood-frame over parking

Further reading

Urban Land
vol. 51, no. 8, 1992 Aug, pp. 40-41
Text in English

Sandy & Babcock International

Bella Vista Apartments

California, USA
1992

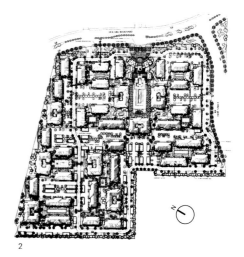

1

community atmosphere.

The project is close to Santa Clara's commercial centre and the City planning authority placed three critical requirements on the design - high density, a minimum parking ratio of 1.8 to 1 and 45% of the site to remain as open space. The Master Plan achieves these by clustering the buildings in small groups, each focusing on a mini park or "common", linked together by a loop road and footpath network. The City Planning Authority also imposed a limit of three-storeys to avoid the buildings overpowering their surroundings. Five building types were developed using eleven dwelling plans in two and three storey buildings. The varied roof heights create a random silhouette, which adds to the character of the scheme. The parking ratio was achieved through providing spaces below some of the buildings and in lock-up garages integrated into the built form.

The focal point and heart of the complex is a 9,000 square foot (837 sq m.) recreation building. This is situated on an axis with the large central pool, providing sweeping views of the hills beyond. The graceful arcade façade of the building's east side welcomes visitors to the project.

The dwellings are spacious and planned with fully fitted kitchens complete with washers and dryers and luxury bathrooms. Externally the lush landscaping creates communal garden spaces and is designed to give privacy to individual dwellings.

2

1   General view
2   Site plan
3   View of Clubhouse with pool

5

6

4   View from central park with pools
5   Walk way
6   Exterior view

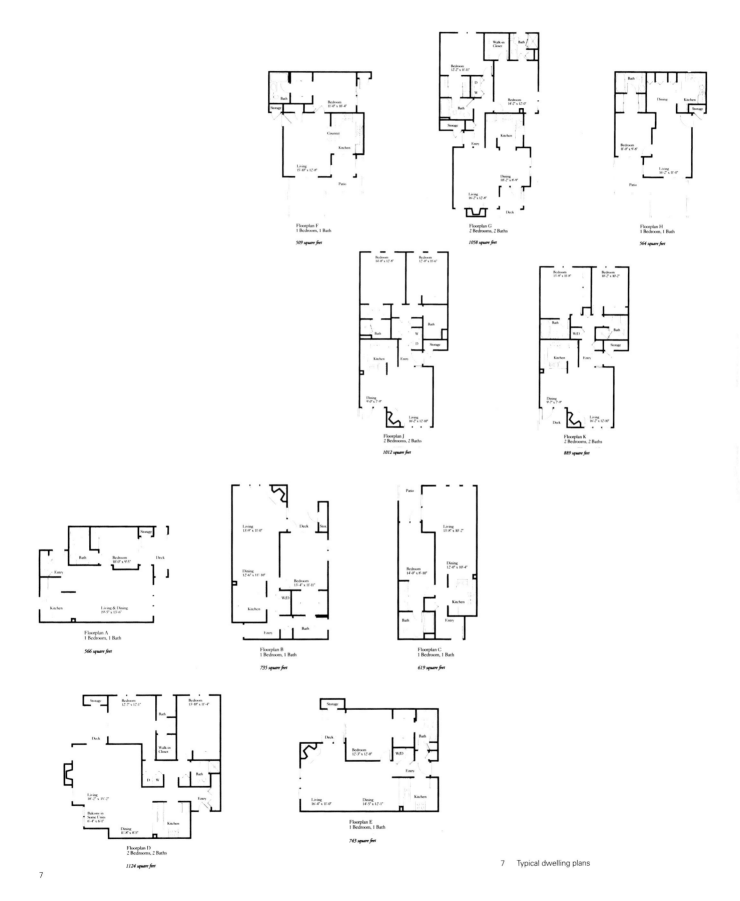

Floorplan F
1 Bedroom, 1 Bath

509 square feet

Floorplan G
2 Bedrooms, 2 Baths

1058 square feet

Floorplan H
1 Bedroom, 1 Bath

564 square feet

Floorplan J
2 Bedrooms, 2 Baths

1012 square feet

Floorplan K
2 Bedrooms, 2 Baths

889 square feet

Floorplan A
1 Bedroom, 1 Bath

566 square feet

Floorplan B
1 Bedroom, 1 Bath

735 square feet

Floorplan C
1 Bedroom, 1 Bath

619 square feet

Floorplan D
2 Bedrooms, 2 Baths

1124 square feet

Floorplan E
1 Bedroom, 1 Bath

743 square feet

7   Typical dwelling plans

7

Chapter 2
Density: 30 - 49 Dwellings Per Acre

The project is situated along one of Ankara's busiest highways and is surrounded by a network of dense and disordered settlements. In contrast, this terraced housing project has been arranged as building blocks around an outdoor courtyard. The project provides 100 dwellings in 15 housing blocks and includes communal areas and shopping, sauna and parking facilities. The design concept alludes to the typical Cappadocian townscape of houses set in the slopes of a natural valley. This is reinforced by the massing of building pattern to emphasise the grouping of buildings rather than individual dwellings. This is in character with the typical Cappadocian "neighbourhoods" where grouped buildings form a coherent urban framework, which is integrated carefully into the existing natural

Credits & data
Location: Turan Gunes Bulvari, Oran Yolu,
   Ankara, Turkey
Number of dwellings: 100
Site area: 1.2 ha (3.3 acres)
Density: 83 dwellings /ha (34 dwellings/acre)
Parking: Underground parking
Structure: Concrete

Merih Karaaslan, Nuran Karaaslan, Mursit Gunday

Suruculer Terrace Housing

Ankara, Turkey
1995

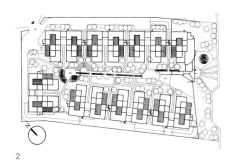
1

context. The colouring of the exterior walls strengthens the "valley" theme and the dominant use of green ensures continuity between the landscape and the building blocks.

As in the ancient towns of Hattusas and Alacahoyuk, the entrance to the "valley" is emphasised by two columns. Shopping and communal activity take place around the entrance. A pedestrian alley runs through the abundantly green outdoor space and terminates in a square encompassing a fountain, obelisk and an open-air amphitheatre. As all car parking is underground the valley is left entirely for pedestrian use.

The design is highly innovative, presenting a critical solution to creating urban housing forms in densely populated areas in this part of the world.

Further reading
SD
no. 7(346), 1993 July, pp. 14-15
Text in English & Japanese

Tasarim
Vol. 3, no. 19, 1991 Dec., pp. 54-83
Text in Turkish. Summaries in English (p. 142)

2

1   View of entrance
2   Site plan

3

4

3   Model: aerial view
4   View of courtyard side
5   Landscape courtyard with pools

6

7

8

6 Exterior view along the street
7 Terrace
8 Interior view of living room
9 Section
10 Elevation
11 Plans

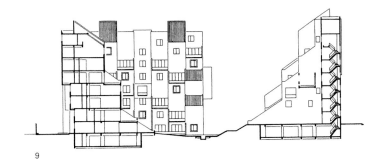

9

10

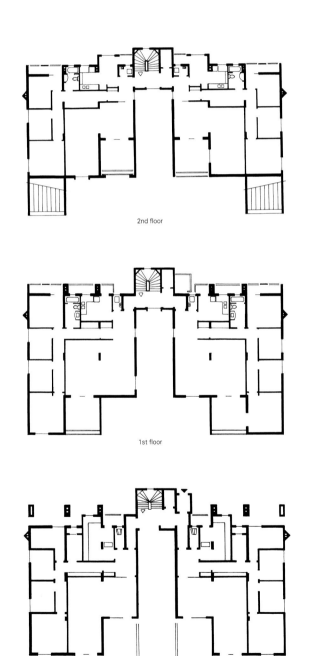

2nd floor

1st floor

Ground floor

11

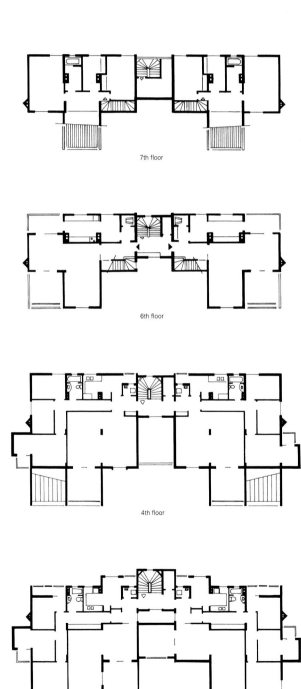

7th floor

6th floor

4th floor

3rd floor

Atelier 5 made a most significant impact on housing design during the second part of the last century. Seidlung Halen built on a wooded hillside site in Berne in 1961 was designed on the principle of the linear stepped-section, narrow fronted, terraced housing block. This was based on Le Corbusier's concepts and was to appear in later years in hillside housing design in many countries, including Britain.

Seidlung Ried 2 was developed out of the architects' own criticism concerning the lack of flexibility in the basic organisation of the long terraces. The scheme has a total of 17 dwelling types to meet the diversity of need. These are arranged around two courtyards. On the north and west sides the housing is in three-storey form and on the east and south

Credits & data

Location: Niederwangen, Bruggbuhlstrasse, Bern, Switzerland
Number of dwellings: 93
Other accommodation: 11 studios / commercial spaces
Site area: 1.27 ha (3.1 acres)
Density: 73 dwellings/ha (30 dwellings/acre)
Typical dwelling sizes:
    1-bedroom flats: 38-43m² (408-462ft²)
    2-bedroom flats: 58-68m² (624-731ft²)
    3-bedroom flats: 82-103m² (882-1,107ft²)
    4-bedroom flats: 112-119m² (1,204-1,279ft²)
Parking/garages: open parking spaces and underground garages
Structure: Reinforced concrete

Atelier 5
Siedlung Ried 2
Bern, Switzerland
1991

1

side it is four-storeys high. Two freestanding corner tower buildings are five storeys high. The dense spatial atmosphere of the courtyard has a near-monastic stamp.

From the courtyard there are various means of access into the dwellings - direct into the maisonettes and via open staircases to the dwelling towers at the corners and to the flats above on the second floor. To break up direct sightlines between dwellings, the housing on the ground floor is raised above the level of the courtyard. This is further assisted by details of facades facing the courtyard such as window screen and blinds, which are designed to provide privacy.

The scheme also includes clubrooms, workshops, sports areas and other communal facilities. Extra studios in the basement are assigned to some apartments.

Further reading

A&U Special issue. Atelier 5, 1976-1992
no. 1 supplement, 1993 Jan., pp. 142-151
Text in English & Japanese

Werk, Bauen & Wohnen
vol. 78/45, no. 6, 1991 June, pp. 34-38
Text in German

Architecture Today
no. 51, 1994 Sept., pp. 14-15
Text in English

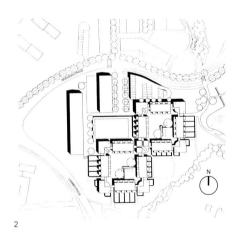

2

1   South façade
2   Site plan
3   General view from the south

3

4

5

4   Exterior view
5   View on the courtyard

6

7

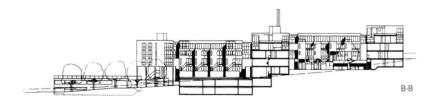

B-B

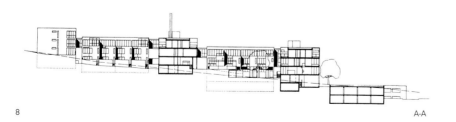

8   A-A

6   View on the courtyard
7   Exterior detail
8   Sections

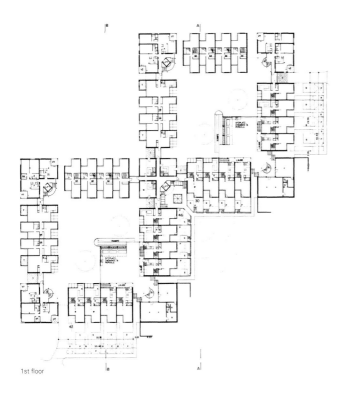

1st floor

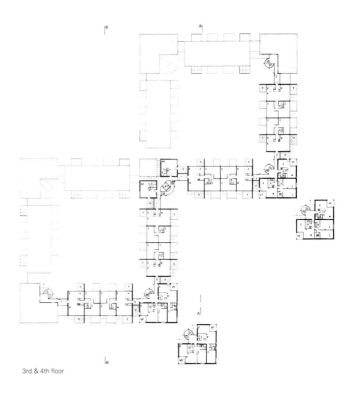

3rd & 4th floor

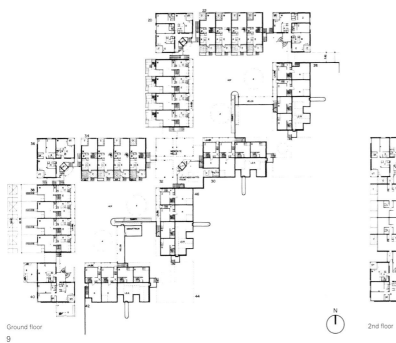

Ground floor

9

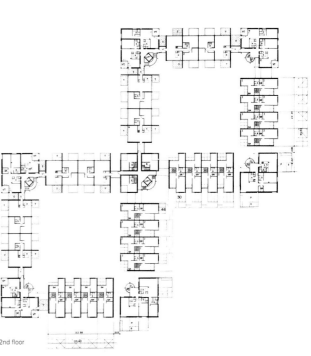

2nd floor

This small but distinguished project is located 5 kilometres (3 miles) east of Tower Bridge. It was built on a site within the London Docklands development area that formerly contained four-storey walk-up flats built around 1930.

The scheme consists of two rows of three-storey terraced houses set at right angles to each other. An additional freestanding building containing 2-bedroom flats helps frame a landscaped courtyard, which is elegantly finished with block paviors, walls and planting. The northern terrace consists of 3-bedroom houses and the western terrace has 4-bedroom houses. At the end of both terraces is a three-storey group of flats. Access to flats at first and second floors is via private staircases.

Entrance for vehicles into the courtyard is

Credits & data

Location: Holyoake Court, Bryan Road, London, UK
Number of dwellings: 25
Dwelling types:
Houses
    3-bedroom houses: 8
    4-bedroom houses: 6
Flats
    2-bedroom flats: 9
Site area: 0.34 ha (1.4 acres)
Density: 74 dwellings/ha (30 dwellings/acre)
Structure: Load bearing brickwork/blockwork

Corrigan + Soundy + Kilaiditi

Holyoake Court

London, UK
1987

1

from Rotherhithe Street and there are two separate footpath entrances. The houses all have integral garages with main living space and kitchen/dining rooms above on the first floor. Additional parking spaces are provided in the courtyard. At the rear of the houses there is a staircase leading down from a balcony on the first floor into the garden.

The exterior design and materials is characteristic of traditional London housing with the splendid use of red, blue and yellow brickwork. The two-storey high bay windows, which face the courtyard at an angle of 45 degrees, give the living rooms more than adequate lighting as well as broad panoramic views. The height, shape and various angles of these windows externally creates a sense of scale in the courtyard that reflects the best quality of a typical London residential street.

Further reading

Building
vol. 253, no. 24, 1988 Jun, pp. 41-48
Text in English

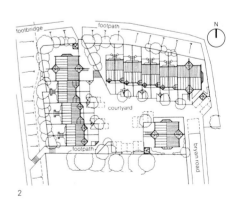

2

1   View on the courtyard
2   Site plan

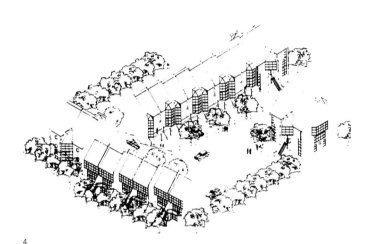

4

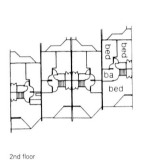

2nd floor

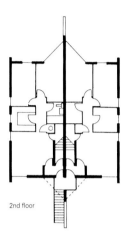

2nd floor

5

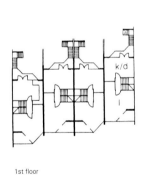

1st floor

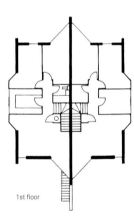

1st floor

6

7

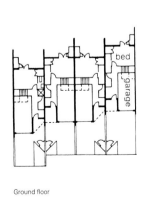

Ground floor

4-bed house

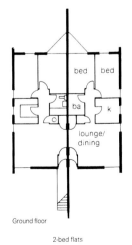

Ground floor

2-bed flats

The architectural world has been excited for some time by the housing work in Graz of the architectural practice, Szyszkowitz-Kowalski, which is most ingenious, particularly their exploitation of the site to give individual character to each project.

At Sandgasse, the housing is arranged in an L-form creating a framed court that acts as an appendage to the nearby park adjoining the scheme. At the same time, the grouping of dwellings forms an urban space that can be perceived as belonging in the private residential realm. The three-storey block along the street consists of flats just above ground level and maisonettes over. A four-storey block of stacked maisonettes runs back into the site along its west side, enjoying a westward view. Access to the upper units is by means of a bridging

Credits & data
Location: Sandgasse 17-21, Graz, Austria
Number of dwellings: 27
Site area: 0.37 ha (0.91 acres)
Density: 73 dwellings/ha (30 dwellings/acre)
Typical dwelling sizes:
    1 no x 38m^2 (408 ft^2)
    3 no x 40-50m^2 (430-538ft^2)
    3 no x 50-60m^2 (538-645ft^2)
    3 no x 60-70m^2 (645-752ft^2)
    4 no x 80-90m^2 (860-968ft^2)
    12 no x 90-100m^2 (968-1,075ft^2)
Number of parking spaces/garages:
    18 garages and 9 open parking spaces
Structure: Brick, reinforced concrete

Szyszkowitz & Kowalski

Sandgasse Housing

Graz, Austria
1991

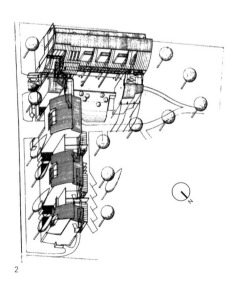

1

structure set well away from the exterior wall of the adjacent housing. Its steel and glass construction provides a light, airy space between the private and public realms. At the same time this bridge provides a place for people to meet.

The colours of the concrete framework and fenestration are bold. Each individual dwelling has a well-defined entrance and clearly legible components such as the box-like protrusions (accommodating dining areas) that also generate variety.

The court is raised about a metre above ground level to accommodate the car parking beneath: the ramps and steps at each end contain the space. It has a built-in seat along the eastern edge and looks down the bank towards the entrance of the flats. This is the heart and social focus, the place for young children to meet and play.

Further reading
Architectural Review
no. 1161, 1993 Nov., pp. 40-44
Text in English

GA Houses
no. 43, 1994 Oct., pp. 148-151
Text in Japanese & English

Deutsche Bauzeitschrift
vol. 41, no. 4, 1993 Apr., pp. 543-550
Text in German

2

1   Entrance of the street from the south
2   Perspective drawing
3   View of the open galleries and the pedestrian court

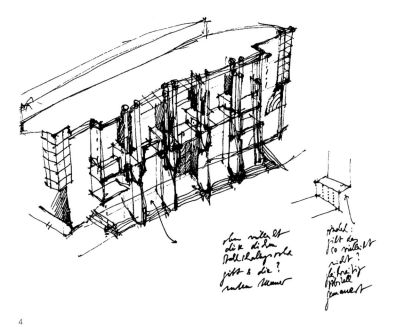

4

4   West side of the west block sketch by the architects
5   View of the south side of the west block

5

6   Top floor of the west block

7   View of the green courtyard

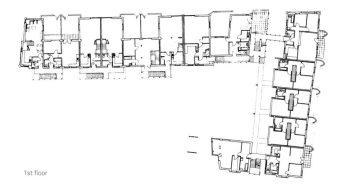

1st floor

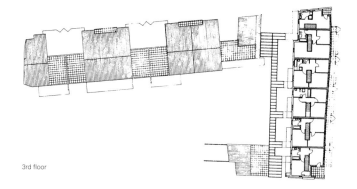

3rd floor

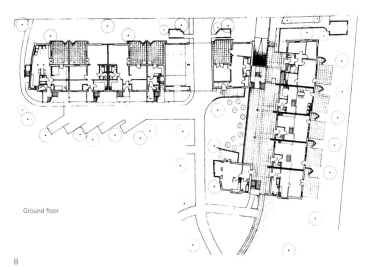

Ground floor

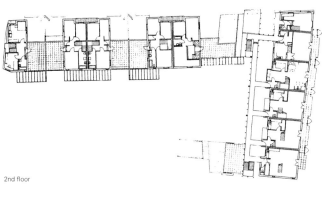

2nd floor

8

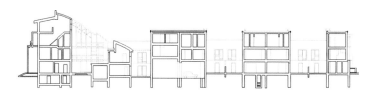

9

8   Floor plans
9   Section
10   Exterior detail

10

The city of Tokyo has many laws and ordinances that restrict the size and scope of housing developments. This can make it difficult for architectural practices to put into practice their theories of designing high quality grouped housing and environments. In this project, however, the architects have cleverly combined the attractions of detachment with the advantages of linked collective housing to form urban courtyard housing with a wide variety of green and open spaces.

The housing is grouped around a linear L-shaped green courtyard with parking beneath reached through the courtyard. It is three-storey in form with two-storey on the southern boundary to allow sun penetration into the courtyard. There are two types of dwelling. The first has a small private garden walled with

Credits & data

Location: 1-32 Kinuta, Setagaya-ku,
    Tokyo, Japan
Number of dwellings: 36
Site area: 0.47 ha (1.2 acres)
Density: 77 dwellings /ha (31 dwellings/acre)
Typical dwelling size: 113m^2 (1,215 ft^2)
Number of parking spaces: 36
Structure: Reinforced concrete

Kojiro Kitayama + K Architect & Associates

Kinuta Terrace

Tokyo, Japan
1991

1

glass blocks. The second has a spacious terrace opening onto the central courtyard. Every dwelling is accessed via a stairwell that opens onto the courtyard.

The most significant feature of the scheme is the design of the courtyard, which suggests new approaches for creating outdoor living space. With the exception of the western block of housing, all front and rear outdoor spaces are designed as part of the courtyard. The result offers a calm alternative to city life outside whilst providing generous open space for children's play. The northern end also links with the local Kinuta Park ensuring a green buffer zone between the housing and the neighbourhood.

Further reading
GA Houses
no. 43, 1994 Oct., pp. 122-129.
Text in Japanese & English

Housing Developments - New Concepts in Architecture & Design, Kunihiko Hayakawa, Meisei Publications, 1994, pp. 131-137
Text in English & Japanese

Nikkei Architecture
1992 July 6, pp. 202-207
Text in Japanese

2

1   Exterior walls on the south

2   Entrance

3

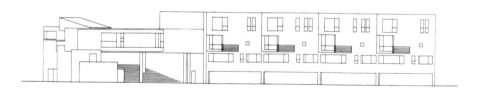

3   Looking into the east courtyard from the entrance
4   Elevations from the east and the west

4

5

6

8

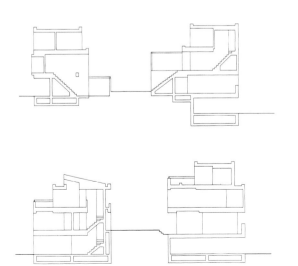

7

5   Looking into the west courtyard
6   Façade on the courtyard
7   Sections
8   Façade detail

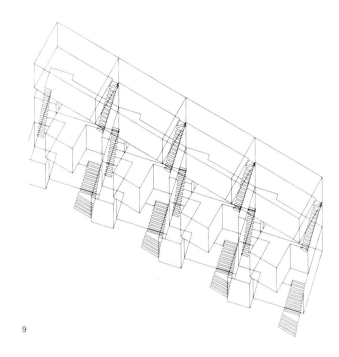

9 Axonometric drawing
10 Plans

9

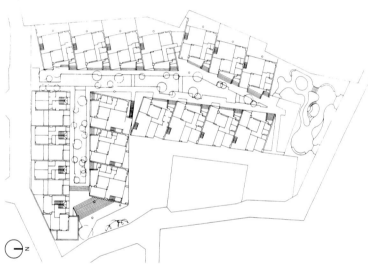

Site + ground floor

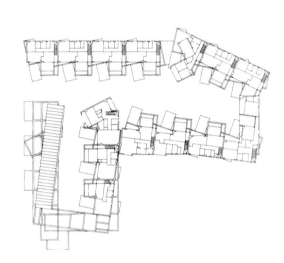

2nd floor

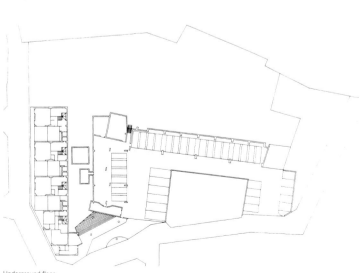

Underground floor
10

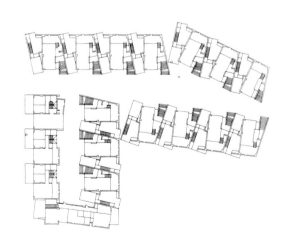

1st floor

The scheme comprises 52 houses in central London arranged around two paved courts which are subdivided by an arch and features within the paved surface, Within this small space are the main elements of traditional town-making-street, courtyard and square. It is a place of delight at every turn; turrets and towers, cast emblems under windows, elegant hopper heads, robust street lighting, the frieze under the arch, and superb ironwork.

The majority of houses are three storeys with a small number of two- and four-storey interspersed. Most have integral garage, porch, hall, cloakroom, kitchen and dining room at ground level, sitting and master bedroom at the first floor and additional bedrooms and bathrooms on the second floor. The house types offer a delightful variety of excitingly

Chapman Taylor Partners

Charles II Place

London, UK
1991

idiosyncratic spaces - a family room with a glazed tower room and weather vane, the studio house with high glazed roof and balcony bedroom, deep turret windows in some living and bedrooms, and tiny, hidden bedroom balconies.

The buildings are a product of traditional brickwork. The obvious care lavished in every detail and the sustained excellence of the workmanship is evident to see. Special bricks enrich the façades including half-round specials to form pilasters to the porch and garage entrances, curved bricks in the slender oriel window towers and special bricks, which enhance the otherwise conventional eaves detail. The rich hues and colours combine with other decorative features to produce a vivid and attractive development in keeping with the artistic traditions of Chelsea.

Credits & data
Location: Charles II Place, Chelsea,
    London, UK
Number of units: 52
Site area: 0.6 ha (1.5 acres)
Density: 87 dwelling/ha (35 dwellings/acre)

1

Further reading
Building
Housing Project Design Awards 1991
vol. 256, no. 7721 (46) supplement, 1991 Nov.
15, pp. 20-21
Text in English

1   Details

2

2   Entrance façade to the courtyard
3   View of the tower on the square
4   Looking into the courtyard

3

4

5

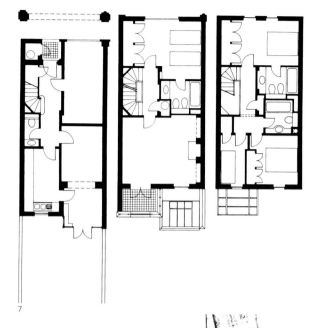

7

6

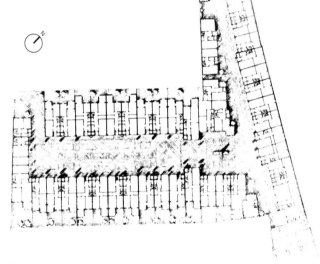

8

9

5 View on the square
6 Exterior detail
7 Typical unit plan
8 Ground floor plan
9 Entrance details

Since the establishment of Kobe as a port in 1868, it has been host to periods of intense foreign settlement, and exposed to many ideas and cultures from overseas. In his master plan for a large site at the foot of the Rokko Mountains, Charles Moore sought to reflect and enhance the image of Western influence on Kobe.

The plan by Charles Moore makes the closest possible connection between the buildings and the landscape. The site was once a rolling hillside with a natural spring but it had been radically graded into flat pads for barrack-like post war housing. The plan involved the restoration of the topography and the grouping of perimeter buildings around a sequence of gardens. It is based on the concept of a formal classical "city" axis between the city and the mountains

Credits & data

Location: Nishiokamoto 2, Kobe, Japan
Number of dwellings: 315
Other accommodation:
    Office space 3,650m² (39,238ft²)
Site area: 3.56 ha (8.8 acres)
Density: 89 dwellings /ha (36 dwellings/acre)
Structure: Reinforced concrete

Moore Ruble Yudell Architects & Planners

Housing in Kobe

Kobe, Japan
1992

1

crossing an informal axis of meandering public gardens running with the topography.

The gardens are a narrative to be experienced either individually or as a continuous journey. A stream rises within the mountain garden, winds through the meadow garden, past a waterfall to rest in the ocean garden. The formal axis leads through a dignified allée of magnolia trees, stops at the waterfall and ends in a quiet white garden. Each space provides individual character to the dwellings that overlook them.

The buildings step up from three to eight floors, with a pair of eleven-storey towers framing the formal axis and serving as a focal point at the crossing of the main axes. The housing is clad in stone, plaster and concrete rising to glazed winter gardens where they meet pitched roofs and dormers.

Further reading

Landscape Architecture
vol. 83, no. 7, 1993 July, p. 29
Text in English

Shinkenchiku
1992 May., pp. 247-256
Text in Japanese

2

1   Exterior view
2   Site plan

3

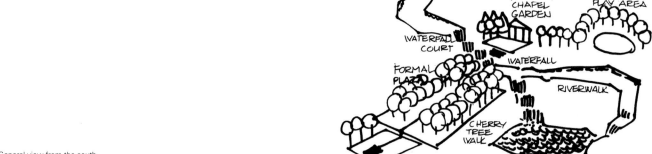

3   General view from the south
4   Landscape study
5   Beautiful landscapes

4

6&7 Views on the central court
8 Interior view of the lobby

6

7

8

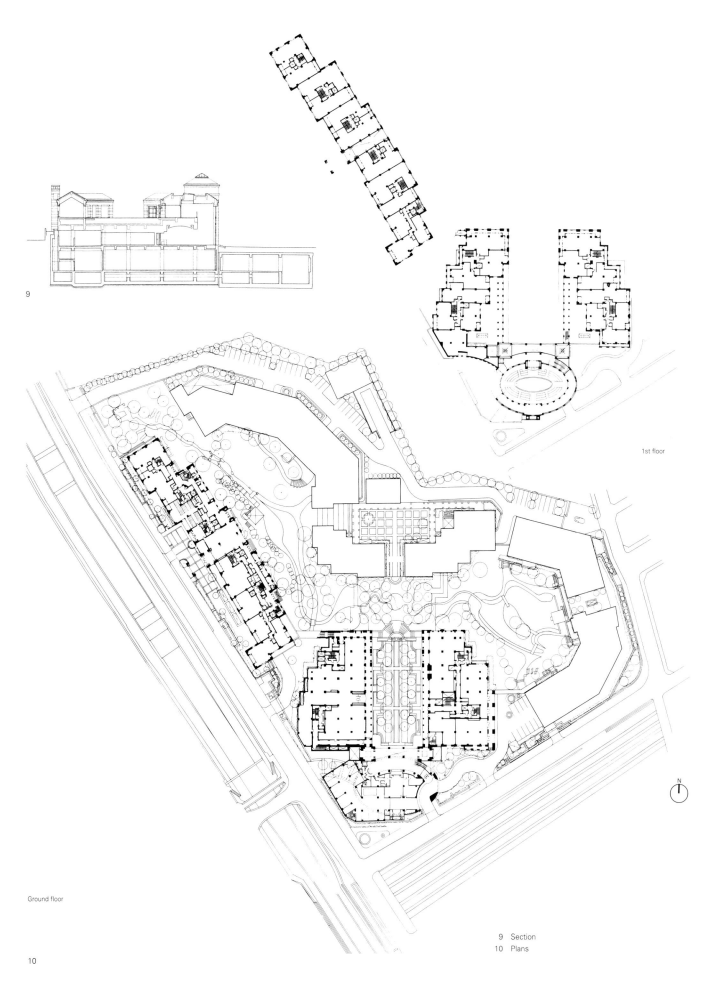

9   1st floor

Ground floor

9   Section
10 Plans

N

10

The redevelopment with apartment blocks of urban sites containing large single houses in a way that does not harm the character of the area is a common problem in many countries. This small housing project illustrates a concept for creating modern day apartments within the form of the traditional Viennese villa. A typological study identified popular elements of the Viennese villa - scale, volume, materials, courtyards, gardens, fencing and the Pawlatschen (open walkways around the courtyard), all of which could contribute to the quality of apartment living if carefully integrated into the design. The architects then considered design solutions that would be in harmony with the neighbourhood.

The built project comprises 2, three-storey apartment blocks clustered on either side of a

Credits & data

Location: Gatterburggasse, Vienna, Austria
Number of dwellings: 19
Site area: 0.21 ha (0.52 acres)
Density: 91 dwellings/ha (37 dwellings/acre)
Typical dwelling sizes:
    6 no x 40m^2 (431ft^2)
    5 no x 54m^2 (581ft^2)
    6 no x 86m^2 (926ft^2)
    2 no x 93m^2 (1,001ft^2)
Parking: Underground garaging
Structure: Concrete

Anton Schweighofer

Urban Villas on Gatterburggasse

Vienna, Austria
1989

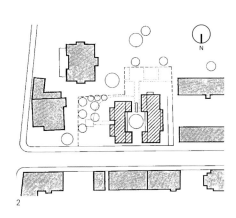

1

small mainly hard paved courtyard. The relationship between solid and void was skilfully handled. Entrance halls were built as winter gardens. Greenhouse-style bay windows facing the courtyard were provided to increase sun penetration, and the extensive use of glass gives a more open atmosphere to the corridors linking the apartments. The tight clustering of the apartments around the courtyard and building the complex close up to the road has left two useful garden areas on the south and east which are nicely equipped with toddlers' play equipment and sitting out space. The design of the landscaping shows an exquisite combination of art and nature. The spatial creation provides sequence, flow, natural space both interior and exterior and a sensitive transition between the two.

Further reading
Casabella
vol. 51, no. 540, 1987 Nov., pp. 38-41
Text in Italian

Werk, Bauen & Wohnen
vol. 76/43, no. 5, 1989 May, pp. 40-49
Text in German

2

1   Exterior view from the street
2   Site plan
3   View of the east wing on the courtyard

4   Plans
5   Section
6   Looking at the courtyard from the entrance
7   Looking at the gardens

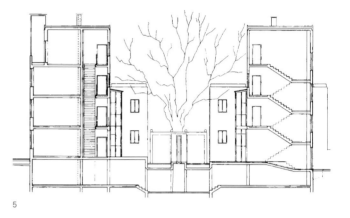

5

6

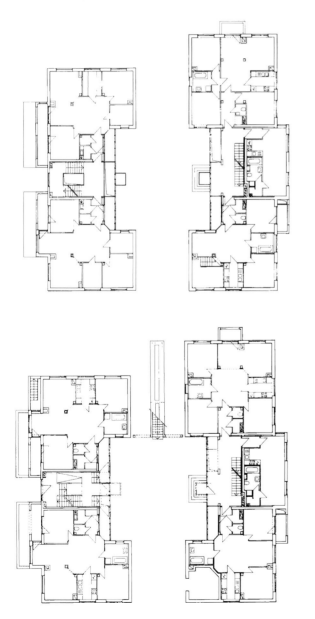

7

4

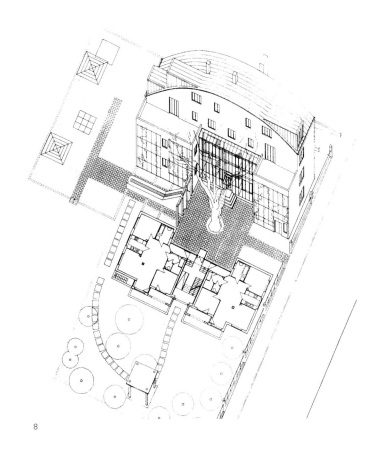

8

8   Aerial view of the west wing
9   View of the courtyard

9

The Ju'er Courtyard housing project retains the essential character of Beijing's Hutong housing. Its apartments are low-rise in form with two- and -three bedrooms, kitchens, bathrooms and central heating providing the essential necessities of modern living. The design achieves a balance between privacy and community life. Courtyards are created by interlocking layouts of various flats, and in creating these courtyards, existing trees, many of which are of historic value, have been preserved. Careful design avoids overlooking between dwellings. Roof terraces provide outdoor or semi-outdoor space, which is far larger than that in conventional apartment blocks. In addition, the loft space under the pitched roofs can be turned into general storage, offices or temporary accommodation for residents whose housing is still under construction.

Credits & data
Location: Ju'er Hutong, Jiaonan Street,
    Dongcheng-ward, Beijing, China
Number of dwellings: 206
Site area: 2.2 ha (5.4 acres)
Density: 94 dwellings/ha (average)
    (38 dwellings/acre)
Typical dwelling sizes: 60-86m^2 (645-926ft^2)
Structure: Brick, concrete

Further reading
Architectural Review
vol. 207, no. 1236, 2000 Feb, pp. 73-75
Text in English

Architectural Journal
no. 2, 1991 Feb., pp. 7-13.
Text in Chinese. Summaries in English (p. 64)

India Institute of Architects Journal
vol. 56, no. 3, 1991 Mar., pp. 31-38
Text in English

Liangyong Wu

Ju'er Hutong Courtyard Housing

Beijing, China
1992

1

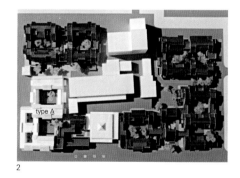

2

The project has shown that, given the fixed two- and three-storey height limit, the courtyard form can achieve the same density as high-rise housing. At the same time, it brings other benefits including a green, quiet environment in the heart of the city and the retention of a socially cohesive community life in the area. Compared to high-rise development, the construction process is simple and affordable and the dwellings have lower maintenance costs.

However, the project is not simply one of physical restoration. It also sought to establish new approaches to the funding provision for housing development in China and better collaboration between local government, residents and academics to create better living conditions in the poorer areas of Chinese cities. The project changed the traditional housing allocation system, under which everyone expects the state to provide them

with free housing, which has proved financially impossible. Instead costs are shared between local government, the residents and the employment units where residents work. Existing residents are entitled to a discounted price to encourage them to stay in the project. Those that do not wish to remain are provided with good quality alternative accommodation. Any flats remaining are sold at full market price, thereby recouping the costs incurred and generating a surplus to enable further work to be carried out.

A further innovation is the cooperation between residents, architects and planners and local government. A housing co-operative has been formally established and is supported by the residents. The Ju'er Hutong experiment is now regarded by Beijing City Government as a model for future development of the historic areas of the city.

1   View of gateway to courtyard
2   Model of site
3   Aerial view

3

4

5

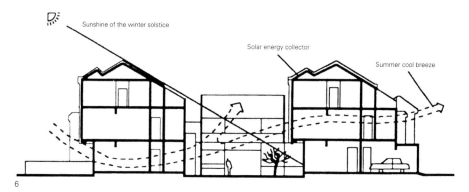

Sunshine of the winter solstice

Solar energy collector

Summer cool breeze

6

4   Model
5   View on the courtyard
6   Studies

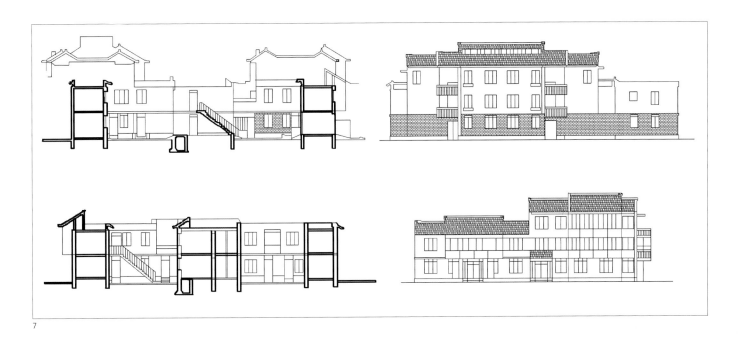

7

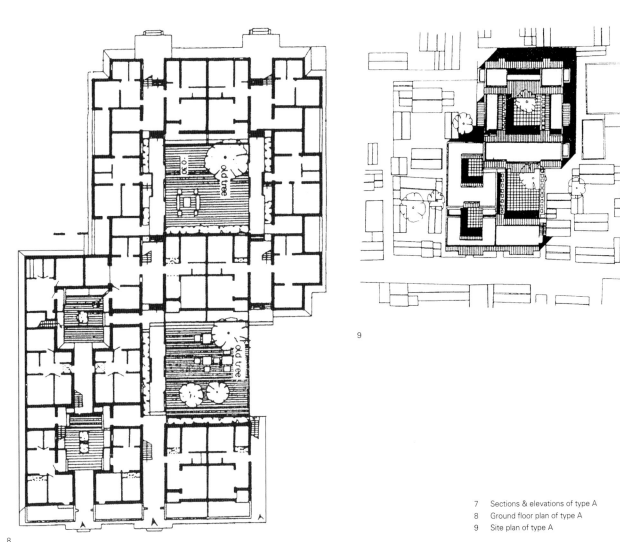

8

9

7 Sections & elevations of type A
8 Ground floor plan of type A
9 Site plan of type A

Delfts Blauw is situated on the edge of the historic city centre of Delft on the site of a former police station. City blocks of buildings with charming internal green courtyards form the character of the area. The occasional alleyways that cut into these blocks are lined with small 2-storey live/work townhouses.

The project reflects the rhythm of this urban fabric with two large, partly linked apartment blocks located along the Westvest canal. These sit at right angles to the block located between the Westvest and Oude Delft canals forming a narrow residential street with town houses. This street and the existing renovated buildings along the Oude Delft canals enclose a green courtyard.

The apartments along the Westvest are elevated above the city streets with shops on the ground floor. Each is a spacious, airy dwelling

Credits & data

Location: Delft, the Netheralands
Number of dwellings: 39
Other accommodation:
  1,000m^2(10,750ft^2) office space
Site area: 0.36 ha (0.89 acres)
Density: 108 dwellings/ha (44 dwellings/acre)

de Architekten Cie. Amsterdam, Frits van Dongen

Delfts Blauw

Delft, The Netherlands
1998

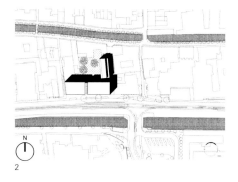

1

on a single floor with attractive views of the town and shared use of the quiet internal courtyard. The town houses also look into this courtyard and have a splendid view over Westvest.

The form of the new development preserves the classic morphology of the city block. It restores traditional urban qualities and fuses a synergy of old and new by modern means. The louvered façades along Westvest are an attempt to impart grandeur. The double-height access corridor is similarly a conscious reflection of modern spatial design not seen in most contemporary housing. As the Architects say in their description: "A subtle play of voids adds a new dimension to the typology of the town house and introduces daylight, air and an open view into the traditional self-enclosed and rather dark town dwelling".

1 South façade of the apartment building
2 Site plan
3 Entrance façade of the apartment building

4

5

4&5   Exterior view from the south

6

7

6 View on the green courtyard from the north
7 View of town houses from the east

8   Section of apartment building
9   Interior view of double-heights access corridor
10 Plans

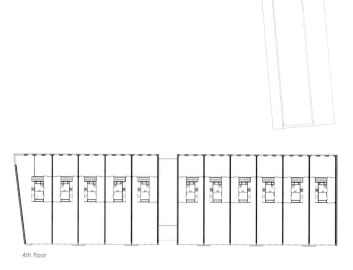

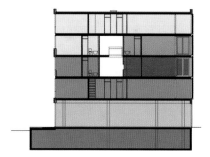

8

4th floor

3rd floor

N

Ground floor

9

10

Georges Maurios won the Rue Balard commission in a limited competition held in 1985 as part of the City of Paris comprehensive redevelopment plan for the former Citroën factory site overlooking the River Seine on the south west of the city, and its 15th arrondissement environment. The City of Paris planners wanted street frontage development, particularly on Rue Balard, but instead of commissioning one architect to design a scheme for the whole site they opted for what was then a new policy, intended to achieve variety, of splitting the site into three component parts for which different architects were appointed. Maurios was given the Balard-Cauchy right angle to design with Prefecture de Police administration staff low rental housing.

Credits & data

Location: 43-47 Rue Balard, 75015 Paris, France
Number of dwellings: 81
Site area: 0.78 ha (1.93 acres)
Density: 104 dwellings/ha (42 dwellings/acre)
Other accommodation:
    $360m^2$ commercial space at street level
Number of parking spaces:
    71 underground parking spaces
Structure: Concrete

Atelier Georges Maurios

Rue Balard Housing

Paris, France
1989

The scheme provides 81 dwellings ranging from one-room flats to seven-room maisonettes with basement car parking, a tenants' meeting room and a row of shops on the ground floor of the Rue Balard frontage. The elevations fronting the two streets are quite different but most interesting is the corner intersection, shaped like a turret, containing a three-storey entrance hall lit by fully-glazed walls to the street and rear courtyard. The effect produced by the design turns the entrance into a hub of communications.

In this scheme George Maurios has rediscovered the composition of traditional cities and architecture, drawing on the experience of Le Corbusier and Louis Khan in his earlier years. He has translated the vocabulary of traditional Parisian architecture, for which the city is so famed, into a modern language.

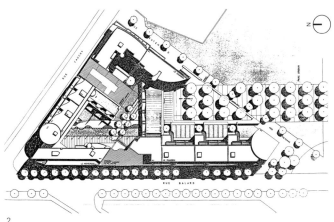

1   Exterior view
2   Site plan

3

4

5

6

3&4 View of the courtyard side
   5 Exterior wall
   6 Entrance

7   Floor plans
8   Section
9   Details

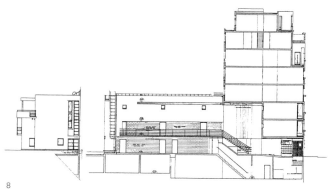

8

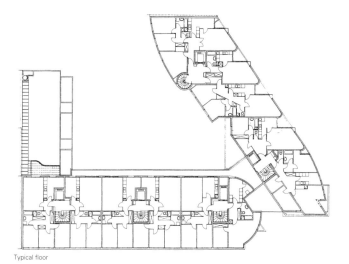

Typical floor

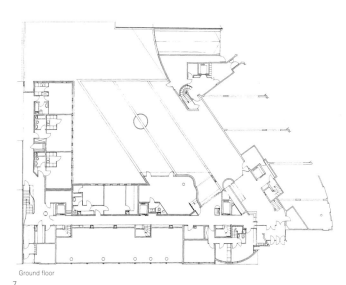

Ground floor

7

9

Yoga A-Flat is situated in a tranquil residential area of Setagaya, Tokyo. It is an experimental collective rental housing project specifically created for artists and designers. The scheme consists of two square-shaped blocks of two-storey housing standing on either side of a semi-enclosed urban courtyard, which contains stairs and a catwalk at first floor level. A third block, which hovers over the entrance at second floor level, links the two blocks and forms a gateway into the courtyard. The screened wall facing the courtyard is designed to take the household equipment. This provides a polished, yet concise character for the façade. The courtyard is full of chairs and tables and is much enjoyed as a communal space by the residents.

The scheme contains eight housing units,

Credits & data
Location: 3-1-17 Kamiyoga, Setagaya-ku,
    Tokyo, Japan
Number of dwellings: 8
Site area: 0.07 ha (0.17 acre)
Density: 114 dwellings/ha (46 dwellings/acre)
Typical dwelling size: 70m² (753ft²)
Number of parking spaces: 5
Structure: Reinforced concrete

Kunihiko Hayakawa Architect & Associates

Yoga A-Flat

Tokyo, Japan
1993

1

each formed as a standard box containing two dwellings, and measuring approximately 4.5m (14ft. 8ins.) in height. There is communal hall at basement level, which can seat more than 50 people.

The dwelling design reflects the growing challenge to the designers of modern housing to provide, through the creation of open, continuous space, flexible forms of housing that can accommodate a growing diversity of lifestyle. In this project each house has its own individual plan that relates to the particular household need but the design allows for the possibility of change. Even bathrooms and kitchens are designed with moveable units on wheels. They are no longer considered to be fittings and fixtures but rather a part of the household's equipment that can be arranged in any way to suit the user's requirements.

Further reading
GA Houses
no. 38, 1993 July, pp. 150-165
Text in Japanese & English

Japan Architect
1994 spring, no. 13, pp. 200-203
Text in Japanese & English

Kenchiku Bunka
1993 July, vol. 48, no. 561, pp. 81-95
Text in Japanese. Summaries in English

1   General view

2   View of the street facade
3   Axonometric drawing
4   Passages on the 1st floor

3

4

5

5   Looking at the court towards the entrance
6   View of the court from the entrance

6

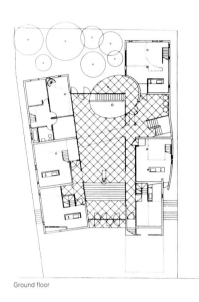

Ground floor

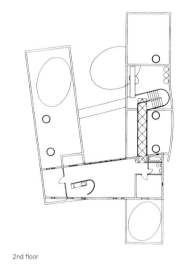

2nd floor

7   Plans
8   Sections

Underground floor

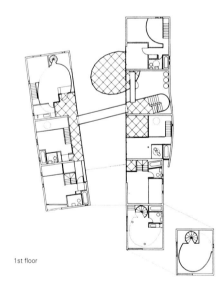

1st floor

N

7

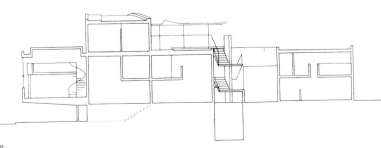
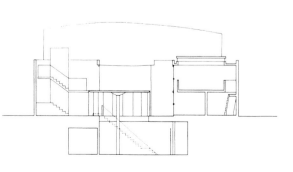

8

During the last 20 years the face of the River Thames has changed dramatically as new housing projects have demonstrated the success of the London Docklands regeneration. Situated to the west of Canary Wharf in a visually strategic location on an outer bend of the River Thames, Dundee Wharf presented a rare potential for exploiting views both upstream and downstream, and, in addition, making a strong statement in the riverscape.

The building form expresses the bend in an eleven-storey tower with a two-storey opening beneath on the river's edge and two wings of seven-storey flats on either side facing up and down stream. The wings step down to three-storeys along Limekiln Dock and Three Colt Street in response to the scale of neighbourhood buildings. This irregular

CZWG Architects
Dundee Wharf
London, UK
1997

Credits & data
Location: Three Colt Street, Limehouse,
    London, E14, UK
Number of dwellings: 132
    Apartments: 127
    Houses: 5
Site area: 1.11 ha (2.75 acres)
Density: 119 dwelling/ha (48 dwellings/acre)
Number of parking spaces/garages: 43
parking spaces and underground garaging

1

"horseshoe" of buildings contains the private court at the rear of the development. All accommodation is accessed from this side by means of a simple loop road, defining a coherent self-supervised urban space. The flats are some of the largest in Docklands, each filling a whole floor of the angle block.

The vocabulary of quayside engineering is dramatically expressed in the project. Crane-like "V" shaped attachments, that take their form from ships' loading booms, support balconies along the river façades. At the angle of the development the eleven-storey tower is complete with a freestanding steel "oil rig" tower of large balcony decks linked by bridges to the tower apartments. The result is a very powerful architectural expression. In front is a very fine footbridge by YRM/Anthony Hunt Associates completed in 1995.

Further reading
Architectural Review
vol. 204, no. 1222, 1998 Dec., pp. 54-57
Text in English

RIBA Book of 20th Century British Housing
Colquhoun, I., Architectural Press/
Butterworth Heinemann, 1999, pp. 135-136
Text in English

Building
1997 Nov., Brick Awards, p. 52
Text in English

1   Looking up the tower

2

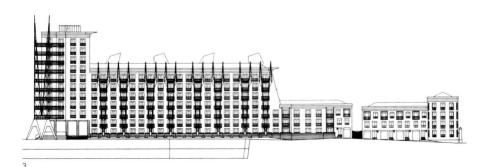

3

2   General view
3   South elevation facing River Thames

5

6

4   North exterior view facing the dock
5   Exterior façade
6   Exterior detail

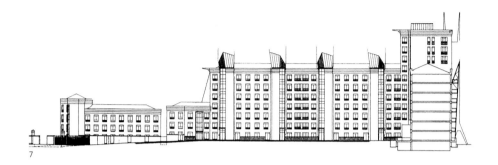

7

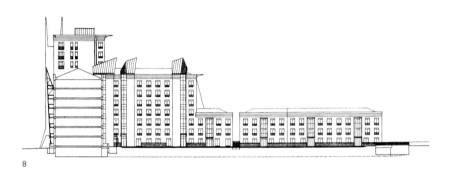

8

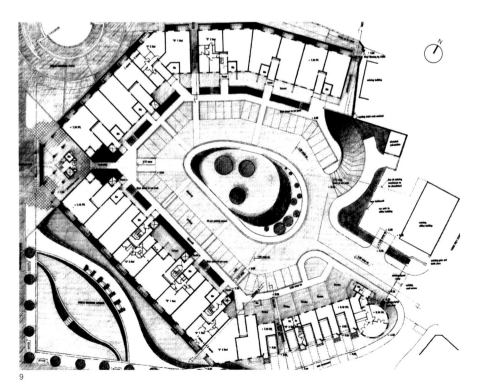

9

7　　North elevation facing the courtyard
8　　South elevation facing the courtyard
9　　Ground floor plan

One of the most critical problems that Japan has carried over into the 21st Century is the proliferation of disorganised developments that bear little relationship to one another or their surroundings. This is even a problem in rural areas that are famed for their natural beauty where the scenery has been fatally destroyed by the sprawl of universal roadside commercial developments. The design of this project, located at the foot of Mount Fuji on the periphery of Shizouka, some 200km southwest of Tokyo, attempted to propose an alternative approach that would be aesthetically acceptable whilst financially and ecologically feasible.

The brief for the project was to develop a 0.10 hectare (0.25 acre) privately owned site situated in a dispersed residential area, patched with remaining paddy fields and with housing comprising 12, 2-bedroom apartments with car parking for all dwellings. Although the project

Credits & data
Location: Nakajima, Fuji city, Shizuoka, Japan
Number of dwellings: 12
    Houses: 50
    Flats: 6
Site Area: 0.10 ha (0.25 acres)
Density: 120 dwellings/ha (48 dwellings/acre)
Typical dwelling size:
    2-bedroom: 60m^2 (646ft^2)
Number of parking spaces: 12

Further reading
GA Japan
no. 38, no. 1, 1999 May., pp. 134-141
Text in English & Japanese

Sinkenchiku
1999 Jun., pp. 207-212
Text in Japanese

Yasumitsu Matsunaga / Modern Architecture Institute

Nakajima Garden Housing

Shizuoka, Japan
1999

1

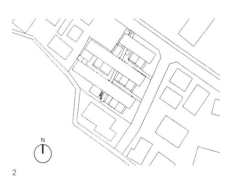

2

was partially subsidised by the government, the costs had to be kept to a minimum. The introduction of modern architectural theory to Japan brought with it the concept of mid-rise, walk-up, flat slab blocks, which often seem alien to their surrounding environment. They offered improved housing at the time but are now unpopular with residents, many of whom are reaching old age.

This project marks a departure from past ideas to low rise/high density housing with building heights kept to two storeys to enable the development to merge into its surroundings. Optimum exposure to sunlight in the winter is achieved by placing the blocks in parallel rows to face south, and natural cooling in the summer was made possible by cross ventilation. Flats are located at the eastern part of the development and family houses on the west. To reflect the increasing interest in Japan for

gardening, each unit is provided with its own outdoor space either at ground level or on the roof. Narrow lanes flanked by water pumped up from a well beneath the ground run between the blocks. A bridge that crosses the lanes at first floor level links the three rows of housing. The scheme was well planted but this has been added to by profuse resident planting. The area is now very green and has become a sanctuary for wildlife as well as for residents.

1   Patio and pond with cast-in bench at back and bridge above
2   Site plan

3

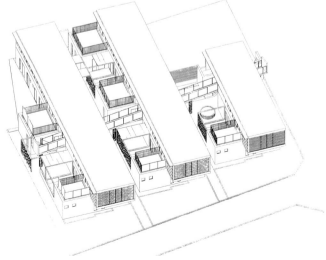

3　East elevation with Mt. Fuji behind and parking in front
4　Axonometric drawing
5　Night view of alley

4

6

7

8

9

10

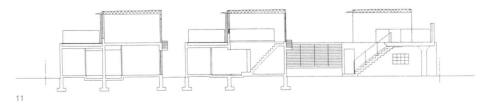

11

6 Patio with bamboo tress
7 Roof gardens comprise the second surface above
   the ground
8 Living room of a first floor flat
9 1st floor plan
10 Ground floor plan
11 Section

Chapter 3
Density: 50 - 69 Dwellings Per Acre

This superb IBA scheme shows a remarkable degree of design ingenuity by Herman Hertzberger's office. The site is located at the end of a triangular area of land. In the corner is a church, which the architects in their design for the housing cleverly left alone to relate to the surrounding buildings.

The project contains 48 dwellings in three- and four-storey blocks grouped around a semi-circular courtyard. The ratio between the distance of one block to the next in height is calculated to ensure ample sunshine in the courtyard during spring and autumn, as well as in summer, while the courtyard is sized in such a way that sufficient space is allotted for a garden area and reasonably large playground facilities for children. The housing was handed over at a stage when the space within the

Credits & data

Location: Lindenstrasse 82-84, Berlin, Germany
Number of dwellings: 48
Dwelling types:
    2-bedroom flats: 6
    3-bedroom flats: 39
    4-bedroom flats: 2
    5-bedroom flats: 1
Site area: 0.37ha (0.94 acres)
Density: 126 dwellings/ha (51 dwellings/acre)
Number of parking spaces/garages: 28 parking garages beneath the courtyard

Herman Hertzberger

Housing on Lindenstrasse

Berlin, Germany
1986

1

courtyard was incomplete so that the tenants could gain a sense of ownership through participating in the design.

The staircases that link the flats illustrate Hertzberger's ideas about common stairs. The use of double front doors allows a side window in the kitchen to overlook the stair when the outer door is open. This allows parents to check that children playing on the stairs are alright. It also means that a traditional anonymous and dirty space is perceived to be an extension of the dwelling. The open staircases double as vertical walkways leading to the terraces or the roofs, which are ideal places for people to meet.

The balconies are spacious and mainly face south. The external face of the scheme presents a graceful yet lively frontage to the surrounding streets, making the project one of the most important in IBA.

Further reading

Architecture d'Aujourd'hui
no. 235, 1984 Oct, pp. 28-31
Text in French

Architectural Review
vol. 182, no. 1085, 1987 July, pp. 63-65
Text in English

GA Houses
no. 23, 1988 Aug., pp. 120-127
Text in Japanese & English

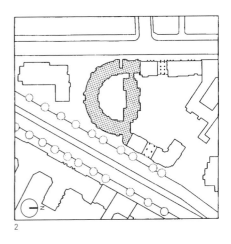

2

1   View of the entrance to the courtyard
2   Site plan

3

3&4 View from the courtyard
5 Children's playground

4

5

6

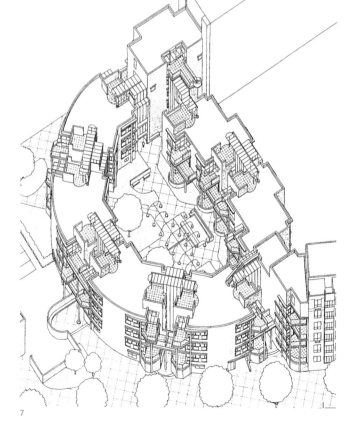

7

6   View of the terraces
7   Pesrpective drawing

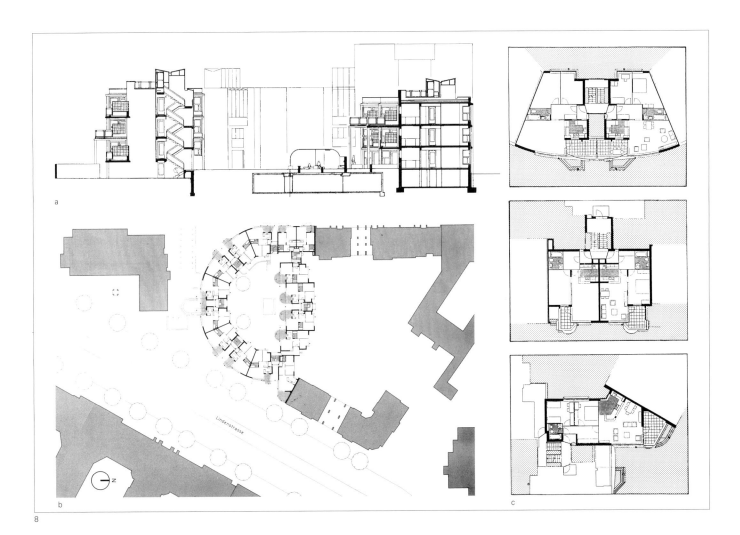

8

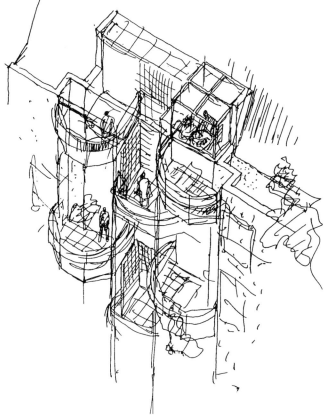

9

8   Drawings
   a Section
   b Ground floor plan
   c Typical apartment types
9   Sketch study

Camden Gardens is a low-cost, affordable rented housing project built on a restricted site in Camden overlooking the Grand Union Canal. There was a planning requirement to preserve three tall trees and the developer, the Community Housing Association, insisted on high density to ensure funding from the Housing Corporation.

The dwellings are distributed between a three-storey terrace of houses and flats along the side of the canal and three, square "villas" containing a mixture of flats and maisonettes facing Camden Gardens. Parking courts situated between villas at the entrance provides the 50 per cent required provision, which frees the centre of the scheme for pedestrian use.

The contrasts of colour between the light yellow bricks, the red screen walls and the

Credits & data

Location: 29-55 Camden Gardens, London, UK
Number of dwellings: 27
    1-bedroom flats: 5
    2-bedroom flats: 6
    3-bedroom flats: 10
    3-bedroom maisonettes: 4
    4-bedroom houses: 2
Site area: 0.2 ha (0.49 acres)
Density: 135 dwellings/ha (55 dwellings/acre)
Number of parking spaces: 14
Structure: Reinforced concrete

1

Jestico & Whiles

Camden Gardens

London, UK
1993

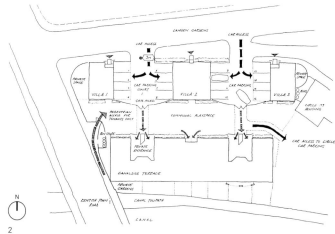

2

brown wooden fencing is most elegantly handled. The appearance of the terrace is characterised by the treatment of the communal stairs. The architects wanted to avoid the bland internal circulation associated with low cost housing schemes so produced a unique solution. A large double-height curved trellis supports the frameless glass canopies, which give the whole area a light and transparent quality. A wide stair passes through the trellis to a deck of timber slats at first floor level, where a second staircase leads up to the upper level. The villas are entered through freestanding portals of terracotta painted masonry.

The layouts of the flats and the large central houses exceed minimum space standards, and all living rooms face south, most with balconies over the canal. Ground floor flats have private garden space.

Further reading

RIBA Book of 20th Century British Housing
Colquhoun, I., Architectural Press/Butterworth Heinemann, 1999, pp. 55-57
Text in English

Architects' Journal
vol. 199, no. 10, 1994 Mar. 9, pp. 45-55
Text in English

Building
Building Homes: Housing Design Awards
vol. 260, no. 7914 (43), 1995 Oct. 27, p. 23
Text in English

1   Entrance façade of the terrace building
2   Concept study + Site plan
3   Looking at the courtyard from the southeast entrance

4   View of the terrace building facing the canal
5   View of the villa building from the street

6 Exploded views: terrace building and villa building
7 Overall view of the courtyard

6

7

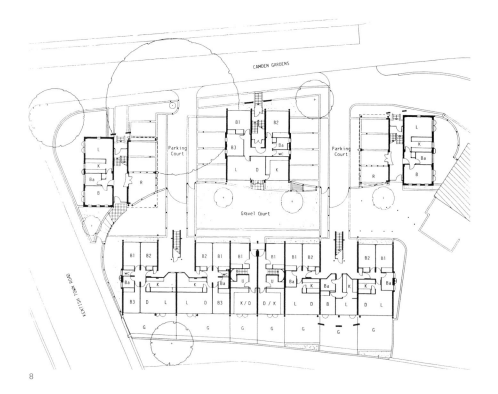

8

9

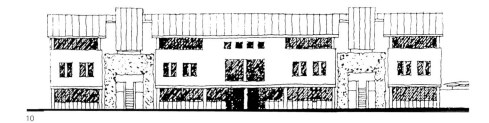

10

8 Ground floor plan
9 Sections
10 Terrace building façade facing the courtyard

This project is located in the suburbs of Tokyo on a slightly sloping site surrounded by detached houses. It was designed to provide a mixture of private rented housing and housing for sale to middleincome people.

The three-storey buildings are grouped around an enclosed courtyard, beautifully designed in traditional Japanese style with gateways, stones and lanterns. Christopher Alexander's "Pattern Language Theory" was used as a rational systematic procedure for the design. The scheme was to be in perfect harmony with the surroundings with dwellings and spaces having a responsive relationship with site levels and existing trees. The project has spacious staircases and galleries with a number of projecting balconies from where residents can linger and enjoy the view of the

Credits & data

Location: 1-16-17 Higashigaoka, Meguro-ku,
    Tokyo, Japan
Number of dwellings: 34
Site area: 0.23 ha (0.57 acres)
Density: 147 dwellings/ha (60 dwellings/acre)
Structure: Reinforced concrete
Number of parking spaces:
    Underground parking

Kohsuke Izumi

Kosugi Housing Project

Tokyo, Japan
1990

1

green courtyard below.

Every dwelling has an individual plan determined by its location on the site and each has its own distinctive features. The majority of sitting rooms face south, with some east-facing exceptions. Most ground floor dwellings on the eastern and southern side of the site have private gardens. Car parking is underground. The architects gave the utmost importance to the choice of materials. Tiles from North Korea, tailor made concrete blocks, soft coloured paints and natural hewn planks all help to create a natural harmony and atmosphere throughout the scheme.

To make the scheme possible the proprietors, architects and lawyers formed a development team, and it took three years to carry out the scheme.

Further reading

Building Homes (Supplement of Building)
Colquhoun, I., "High Society"
24th March 1995, pp 4-7 and cover
Text in English

Nikkei Architecture
no. 21, 1991 Jan., pp. 113-124
Text in Japanese

Shinkenchiku
1991 Jan., pp. 353-359

1   View on the courtyard

2

2   View of the garden
3   View of balconies

4 View of roofs
5 View of access corridor
6 Sections

4

5

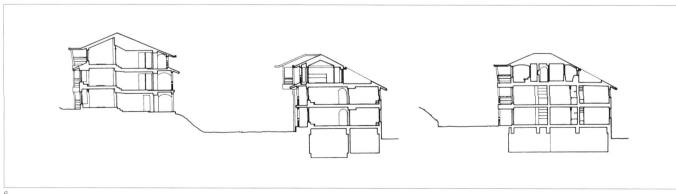

6

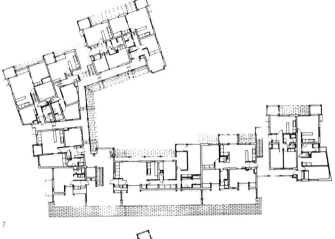

7

7   2nd floor plan
8   1st floor plan
9   Ground floor plan

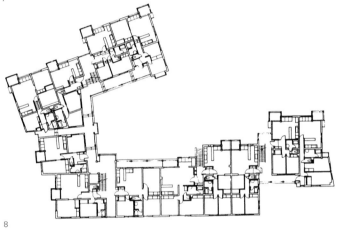

8

9

Style is important in French housing and nowhere is this better illustrated than in the new towns around Paris built between the late 1970's and early 1990's. Amongst the more humane projects, Alain Sarfarti's work was outstanding. Les Glycines in Evry, on the west side of Paris, is traditional but nevertheless highly innovative.

The 103 flats are arranged on either side of a pedestrian concourse and around a communal garden. Access to upper concourse dwellings is gained by spiral staircases, capped with glass umbrellas that would grace the entrance to any Parisian Metro station designed by Hugo Guimand in the early 1900's. The communal garden is delightfully laid out with pergolas and climbing plants, a covered bandstand, sculptures and lush planting of all kinds. Vines

Credits & data
Location: Rue C. Delescluzes, Evry, France
Number of dwellings: 103
Other accommodation:
    270m^2 (2 906ft^2) commercial space
Site area: 0.8 ha (1.97 acres)
Density: 129 dwellings/ha (52 dwellings/acre)
Typical dwelling sizes:
    2-bedroom flats: 75-80m^2 (807-861ft^2)
Number of parking spaces/garages: 116

AREA-Alain Sarfati

Les Glycines

Evry, France
1981

1

and flowers grow luxuriantly. Each house on the ground floor of the concourse has a back garden: those opening onto the communal garden are enclosed by low walls and garden gates. A row of shops is located on the ground floor of the terrace on the further side of the communal garden.

The pedestrian concourse and the dwellings on either side are built above underground garaging. The stripes painted on the tarmac surface create a vivid pattern, which relates to the spiral staircase: at the same time they are a focus for children's play. The rendering on the stucco finishes, brick staircases and blockwork balconies, window proportions, the eaves details that cast a deep shadow across the walls beneath, all create a harmony that reflects in a modern way the essential character of traditional French architecture.

Further reading
Housing Design: An International Perspective
Colquhoun, I., and Fauset, P. GB. T.,
Batsford, 1991, pp. 80-82
Text in English

Architects' Journal
1984 Jan. 25, pp. 46-55
Text in English

Domus
1982 July, pp. 12-13
Text in Italian & English

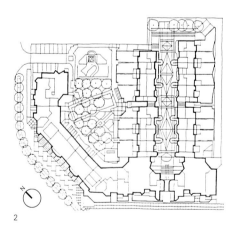

2

1   Pedestrian street view from the south
2   Site plan

3

4

3   Looking into the pedestrian street from the north-east
4   West view of the courtyard

5

6

5-7 Views of the pedestrian street

7

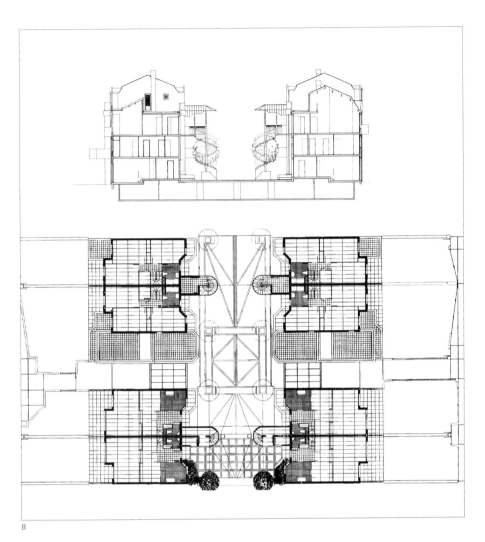

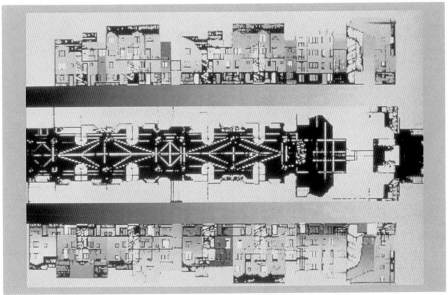

8   Section & typical duplex plan
9   Elevations

This was one of the first urban housing projects undertaken by Danish Architects, Tegnestuen Vandkunsten. The scheme, designed mainly for elderly people, is located on the site of a former shoe factory in Copenhagen. The surviving workshop building on the east side of the project was preserved and converted into housing and the landmark entrance to the factory manager's living is now used as a restaurant.

The project is designed to look inwards towards a courtyard. The building on the west side of the site has been designed as a winding city block receding from the street creating a forecourt with a gateway into the courtyard. On the northeast side, there is a six-storey tower built adjacent to the north entrance of the complex giving an open and dynamic ambiance

Credits & data
Location: Jagtvej 211, Copenhagen, Denmark
Number of dwellings: 71
Site area: 0.5 ha (1.24 acre)
Density: 142 dwellings/ha (57 dwellings/acre)

Further reading
Arkitektur DK
vol. 36, no. 1-2, 1992, pp.16-19
Text in Danish. Summaries in English

Contemporary Danish Housing
Nygaard E, et al., Arkitektens Forlong, 1992,
pp 16-19
Text in Danish. Summaries in English

Guide To Danish Architecture 2
Kim Dirchinck-Holmfeld, Arkitektens Forlag,
1995, pp. 214

Text in English

Tegnestuen Vandkunsten

Garvergarden

Copenhagen, Denmark
1989

1

compared to the narrow entrance on the south.

The most distinctive feature of the scheme is the variation in building heights from two half-storeys on the south to six storeys in the tower. This is a radical departure from the typical Copenhagen city block, but it allows the sun to reach the courtyard. The large sloping roofs, in place of the customary steeped roofs, are also a major departure. The architectural idiom is typically Vandkunsten, with a collage of many different surfaces and colours controlled by an artistic spirit that is so characteristic of the office. Arkitectur DK writes: "Garvergarden is an original and engaged proposal for contemporary urban architectural idioms. Seen from a rational (as opposed to rationalistic) and humanist architectural attitude, it has a special calibre, with a high level of complexity, and many architectural qualities."

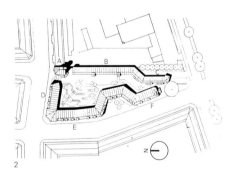

2

1   View of the west building of courtyard side
2   Site plan
3   View of landscaped courtyard

3

4

4   View of the east block of courtyard side

5

6

7

5   Exterior view along the street
6   The north entrance to the courtyard
7   The south entrance to the courtyard

8   South elevation
9   Sections & plans
10 West elevation of street side
11 Elevation of courtyard side seen from east

8

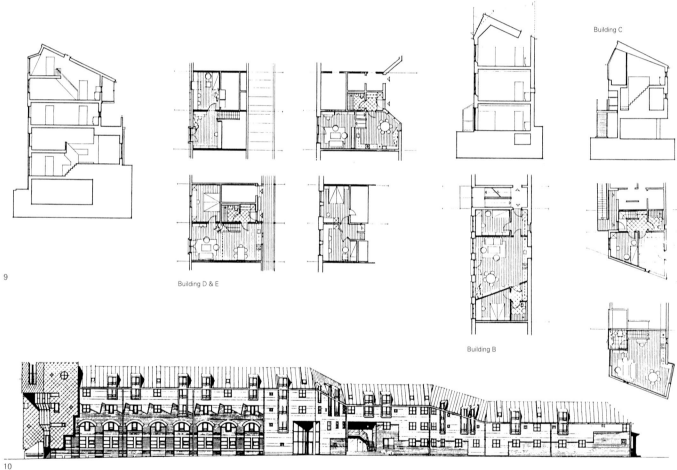

9

Building D & E

Building B

Building C

10

11

The City of Tomorrow

Bo01 is a new sustainable city district of 1,000 dwellings in Malmo, built on land claimed from the sea near the Vastra Hammen (Western Docks). The development was the subject in 2001 of an international exhibition of experimental sustainable housing. Renewable energy is produced locally and supplied to the site. Green spaces are seen as essential to enhance biodiversity within the site and the area uses the most up-to-date eco-technology for the treatment of water and waste.

The site overlooks the sea with wonderful views of the new bridge linking Sweden and Denmark. There is a varied mix of housing ranging from five-, six-, and seven-storey apartments overlooking the seafront, to small sites of low-rise housing, each scheme of which

Credits & data
Location: Boplatsen, Malmo, Sweden
Number of dwellings: 27
Site area: 0.17ha (0.42acres)
Density: 159 dwellings/ha (64 dwellings/acre)
Typical dwelling size: 56-181m^2 (600-1,950ft^2)
Parking: Underground garaging

Further reading
Design Out Crime
Colquhoun, I., Architectural Press, 2004, pp. 253-255. Text in English

Architectural Record
vol. 190, no. 2, 2002 Feb., pp. 156-158
Text in English

Abitare
no. 409, 2001 Sept., pp. 74-78
Text in English & Italian

A&U
no. 6 (381), 2002 Jun., pp. 12-13
Text in English & Japanese

Moore Ruble Yudell Architects & Planners
FFNS Architects

Bo01 - Tango Housing

Malmo, Sweden
2001

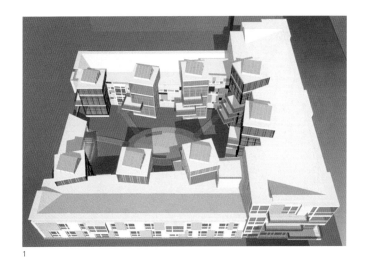

1

was designed by different architects to achieve variety. There is mixed use in the form of shops on the ground floor of the apartments overlooking the seafront and an office area called the "Boplatsen".

Tango Housing

United States Architects, Moore Ruble Yudell, were commissioned to design a small city block of 27 housing units in the Boplatsen. The design concept stemmed from two basic principles:

• Building heights step from four to two floors, enclosing a private oval-shaped courtyard garden, which faces west. On the external perimeter, the architects wanted to relate the block to the surrounding urban fabric and the building form therefore follows the line of the street presenting a private face

with few windows.

• Within the scheme, the living rooms of the individual units are projected into the garden as glass towers to make the living space seem larger. In the evening, when the screens of wood lattice are lit from behind, the glass towers glow like a series of Chinese Lanterns in the garden.

The garden is planted with various kinds of vegetation while recycled water supplies a constant source of beauty and nourishment to the garden.

The architects explain their ideas further as follows: "Dancing around the edge of the garden, the glassy pieces also carry solar panels on top, while stone 'fingers' on the garden wall reinforce a horizontal reading that contrasts with the verticals on the exterior."

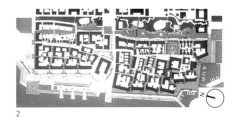

2

1 Aerial view
2 Site plan with block highlighted

3

3   General exterior view from northeast
4   General exterior view from southeast

4

5

6

5   View on the courtyard
6   View of the oval island in garden

7

8

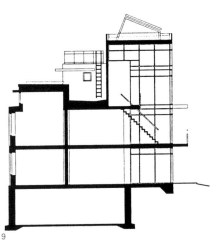

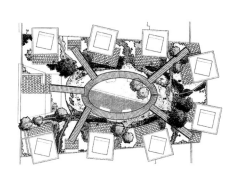

9

10

11

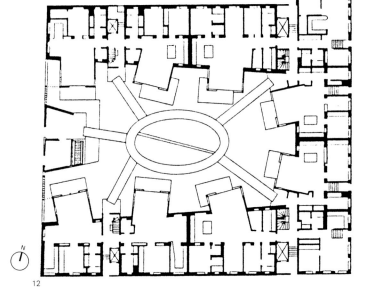

12

7   West façade
8   East façade
9   Section
10 Typical dwelling plan
11 Garden landscape plan
12 Ground floor plan

The redevelopment of Hulme with a mixture of social housing for rent and private housing for sale is one of the most significant regeneration projects in the UK. It is seen as a model for the sustainable urban neighbourhood of the future. The main developers are Bellway Urban Renewal (private housing), and a consortium of housing associations led by the Guinness Trust and North British (social housing for rent). The planning approach was based on the principle of building new housing around a permeable grid of streets to promote sociability, community and natural surveillance. The careful treatment of corners, vistas and landmarks were important as traditional points of reference.

Homes for Change began in 1991 when the Guinness Trust was approached by Hulme residents and small businesses to develop a

Credits & data
Location: 41 Old Birley Street, Hulme,
 Manchester, UK
Number of dwellings: 75
 Phase I: 50
 Phase II: 25
Site Area: 0.53 ha (1.31 acres)
Density: 142 dwellings/ha (57 dwellings/acre)

Mills Beaumont Leavey (Phase I)
Charles Cooper + Harrison Ince (Phase II)

Homes for Change

Manchester, UK
1996 / 2002

1

mixed-use scheme. The first phase comprises 50 flats and maisonettes and 1,500 sq.m. (16,000 sq.ft.) of managed workspace - including shops, offices, a small performance area, which doubles as a meeting room, and a café. This is all accommodated in a six-storey building grouped around a secure central green courtyard overlooked by the open access decks leading to the dwellings. The workspace, built in a shell-and-core format to allow varying sizes and configurations of units, is confined to the two first floors and has external entrances. The dwellings above are reached through the courtyard. Phase 2 completes the courtyard.

The result is a most exciting housing development, which succeeds through the quality of its design and from the formation of a sustainable community right from the beginning.

Further reading
Building
vol. 261, no. 7945, 1996 Sept. 6, pp. 38-43
Text in English

Building
vol. 266, no. 8168 (2), 2001 Jan. 12, pp. 40-45
Text in English

Building Design
no. 1340, 1998 Feb. 27, p. 2
Text in English

Architects' Journal
vol. 205, no. 13, 1997 Apr. 3, p. 34
Text in English

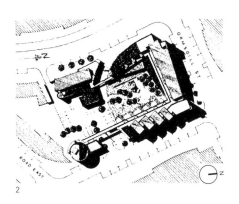

2

1   Exterior view from west
2   Site plan

3

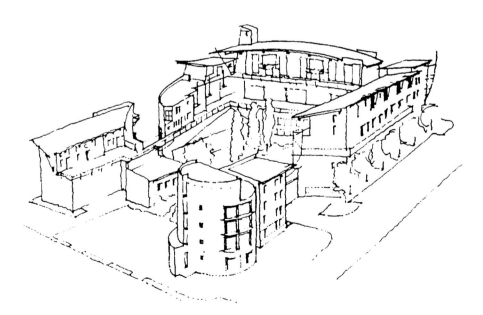

3   View on courtyard from south
4   Perspective drawing
5   West façade of courtyard side

4

6

6   View from the passages in the 2nd floor
7   The café
8   Shop
9   Plans

7

8

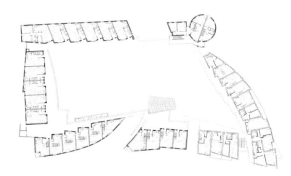

2nd floor

5th floor

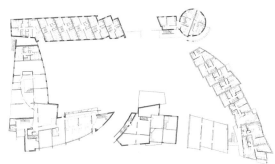

1st floor

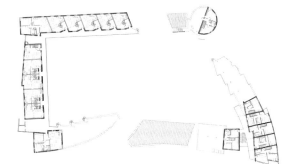

4th floor

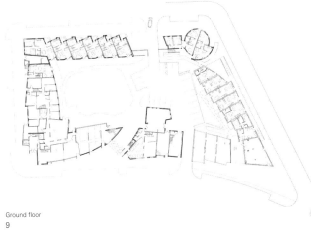

Ground floor

9

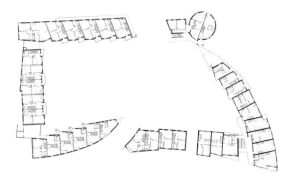

3rd floor

Chapter 4
Density: 70 - 89 Dwellings Per Acre

As its economy develops China is experiencing a huge expansion of its new housing programme, none less than in Shanghai where the Sanliyan Housing Project is situated in the south-west end of the new multi-purpose quarter - the Pudong Development District.

The housing layout draws on traditional Chinese techniques of spatial design. The grouping of apartments takes on the character of the old lanes and alleys in Shanghai. The space between two rows of buildings forms a long courtyard serving as the basic structuring unit of outdoor space. It also continues the traditional Shanghai style of architecture found in old neighbourhoods by using design elements such as Mansard roofs, attics, dormer windows, and houses built with two-storeys above the top floor.

Zhonggu Wang

Sanlinyuan Housing Project

Shanghai, China
1996

1

Most of the new housing is six-storeys in height. The majority contains two bedrooms with an average area of 68 m² (731 sq. ft.). The dwellings on the ground floor are raised on stilts, which prevents flooding during the rainy season. The space beneath the dwellings is used for the parking of cars and bicycles and occasionally accommodates a small grocery store. More importantly the space is used as semi-open space for recreation by children and exercise and fitness by elderly people.

The profusion of greening makes the scheme distinctive. This is in 3 parts - courtyards, group blocks and public green spaces - green lungs - in the centre of the project covering an area of 0.75 ha (1.9 acres). With ponds, fountains and sculptures the overall effect is of a peaceful living environment that is enjoyed by the residents.

Credits & data

Location: Sanlinyuan, Pudong New Area,
　　Shanghai, China
Number of dwellings: 2,092
Site area: 11.9ha (4.8 acres)
Density: 176 dwellings/ha (71 dwellings/acre)
Typical dwelling sizes:
　　1-bedroom: 57m² (613ft²)
　　2-bedroom: 68m² and 72m² (731 and 774ft²)
　　3-bedroom: 84m² (904ft²)
Number of parking spaces:
　　300 spaces for cars
　　300 for motorcycles
　　3,138 for bicycles

1　Model: aerial view of whole complex

2

3

4

2   View on the central park
3   Walkway with pools
4   Exterior view from gardens and walkway

5

6

7

5 Model: aerial view of courtyard blocks
6 Elevation
7 Gateway to the courtyard

8

8 Site plan
9 Typical dwelling plans

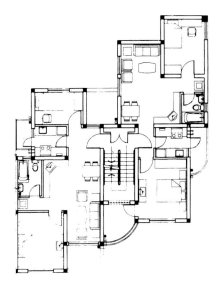

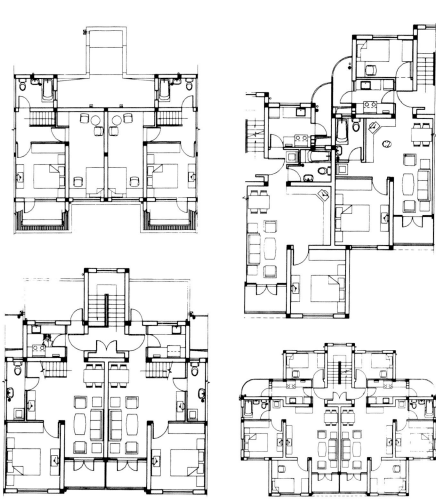

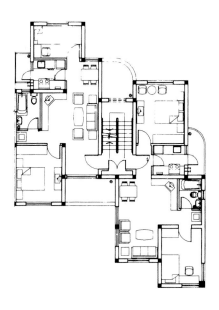

9

Rokko is a man-made island claimed from the sea, linked by a causeway to the mainland and the city of Kobe. The island has been developed to form a new community complete with a varied range of housing, commercial development, business complexes, parkland and open spaces, and other uses. The Rokko planners stipulated that an urban environment be created similar to the downtown area of Kobe. The buildings had to subscribe to an "ocean" metaphor as the unifying design theme, i.e., not enclosed. However, the developers asked for an enclosed community for security and management reasons. To meet these demands, the architect grouped the blocks of housing around a central courtyard accessible only by the residents.

The courtyard is filled with boats, a lighthouse and a children's playground, all designed on the

Credits & data

Location: East Court 5, Rokko Island City,
    Kobe, Japan
Number of dwellings: 191
Other accommodation:
    2 shops and 1 manager's dwelling
Site area: 1.1 ha (2.7 acres)
Density: 174 dwellings/ha (71 dwellings/acre)
Typical dwelling sizes: 65-173m^2 (509-1,270ft^2)
Number of parking spaces: 192
Structure: Reinforced concrete

1

Takao Endo

The Theatre of the Ocean

Kobe, Japan
1990

theme of "The Theatre of the Ocean". A striking feature of the project is the skywalk at third-floor level that unifies the project. This winds and zigzags through the scheme offering the opportunity to appreciate the beauty of the courtyard below from a high level.

The housing around the courtyard comprises single-family apartments in six-storey blocks, an 11-storey block, and a 14-storey block at the head of the group. This contains the main entrance and public facilities including a community centre. The exteriors of the buildings are brightly coloured to relieve the large volume. The triangular roofs are the dominant elevational feature of the scheme.

The courtyard form of layout is rare in Japanese housing but extremely successful because of Takao Endo's ingenious design and perfection of construction.

Further reading

Nikkei Architecture
no. 21, 1991 Jan., pp. 69-76
Text in Japanese

Shinkenchiku
1991 Feb., pp. 346-355
Text in Japanese

1   Details of flyover passages
2   View from the west building

2

3

4

3   View of Northern high-rise building from courtyard
4   View of gateway of southern building along street

5

6

5   General view of the Theatre of the Ocean
6   View of southern multi-storey building from courtyard

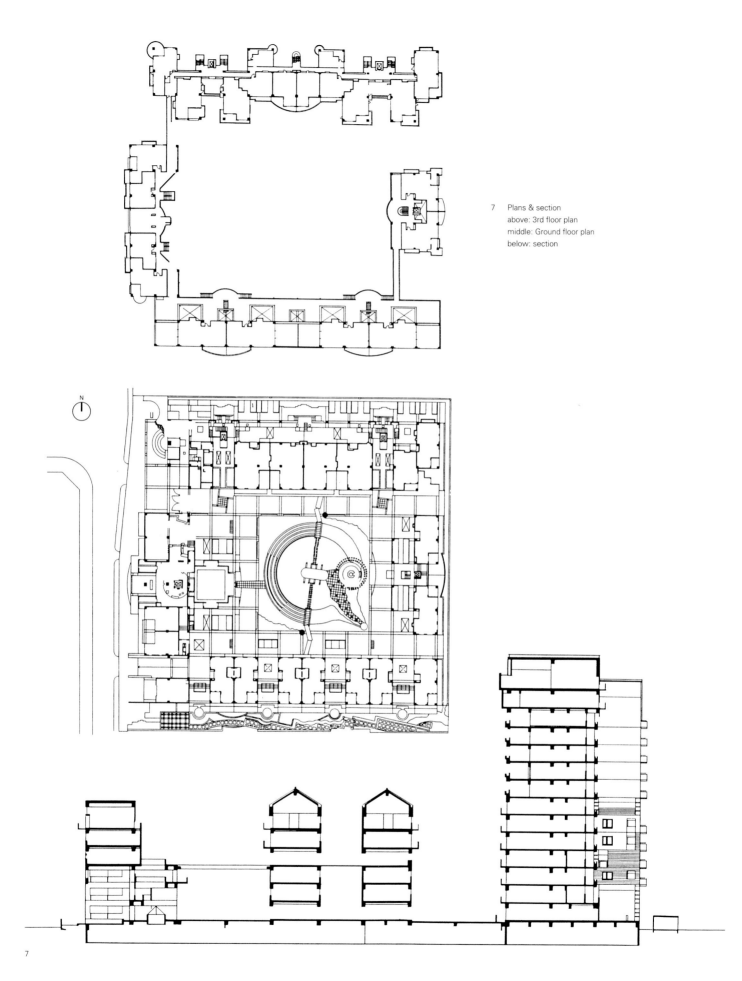

7   Plans & section
      above: 3rd floor plan
      middle: Ground floor plan
      below: section

7

The harbour basins of Amsterdam's eastern docklands were dug at the end of the 19th century but by the 1960's they were disused due to container transport and the increasing size of ships. The plan to redevelop these docklands retains the unique combination of land and water and transforms the former piers into tranquil residential areas. Batavia, which opens out onto an extensive area of water, is a U-shaped housing project built on the site of a former railway yard between Panamalaan, Bomeolaan and Dirk Vreekenstraat. The complex is in five-storey form with a total of 167 dwellings and 1,100m² of business space on the ground floor.

Many of the dwellings have conservatories, which substitute for outdoor space and act as a noise barrier. The conservatories have folding

de Architekten Cie. Amsterdam, Frits van Dongen
Batavia - Entrepot - West 4
Amsterdam, The Netherlands
2000

1

fronts so they can be opened completely in warmer weather. Along Panamalaan they are linked, which gives the impression of a single gigantic window. The business space is also located on this frontage.

There is a considerable variety of dwelling types. Entrance treatments also vary from porticoes on the ground floor, galleries on the fourth floor of the Bomeolaan and Dirk Vreekenstraat sides of the development to corridors on the remaining storeys. The spacious entrance lobbies at the corners of the complex provide access to the corridors and galleries. They offer a wonderful view of the city and at night they form an element of city lighting.

Car parking is semi-underground with patio gardens above. The central courtyard is extensively planted, which gives higher level apartments a lovely view of green space.

Credits & data
Number of dwellings: 167
Other accommodation:
    1,100m²(11,825ft²) business space
Site area: 0.9 ha (2.22 acres)
Density: 185 dwellings/ha (75 dwellings/acre)
Number of parking spaces:
    136 semi-underground parking spaces

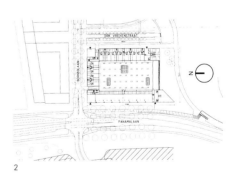

2

1   View from the water
2   Site plan

3

3   Exterior view from northeast
4&5   Exterior view from southwest

4

6

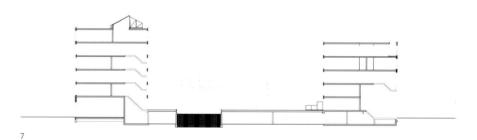

7

8

6   Looking at the courtyard from north
7   Section
8   Looking at the courtyard from south
9   Plans

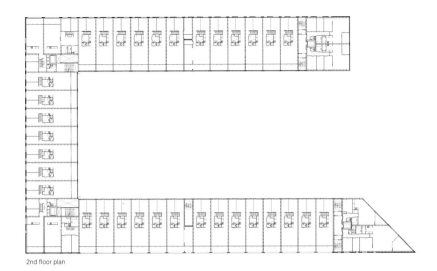

2nd floor plan

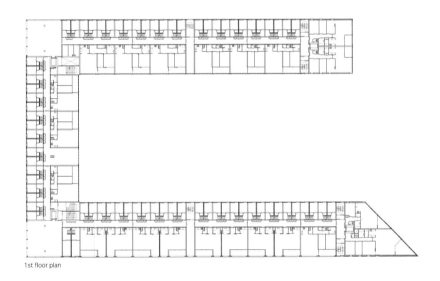

1st floor plan

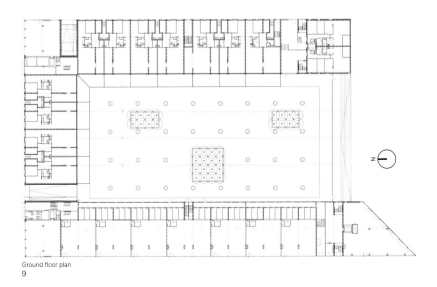

Ground floor plan

9

This complex of 110 housing units and shops was one of the first phases of Makuhari Bay Town, which will eventually accommodate 23,000 residents, business and commercial uses, leisure facilities etc, and a large urban park. The town is situated on a vast area of land reclaimed from the sea around Tokyo Bay. Its design is controlled by a supervisory committee, which legislated strict design guidelines at the inauguration of the project. The streets are laid out in a permeable grid pattern, forming city blocks with buildings of continuous height flanking the streets. In the centre of each block is a landscaped courtyard known as a "patio".

This project faces the main street named "Promenade". The whole of the ground floor was conceived as a platform comprising

Credits & data

Location: 2-4 Utase, Mihama-ku, Chiba, Japan
Number of dwellings: 110
Site area: 0.56 ha (1.39 acres)
Density: 196 dwellings/ha (79 dwellings/acre)
Parking: Underground parking
Structure: Reinforced concrete

Yasumitsu Matsunaga & Kazunari Sakamoto

Makuhari Bay Town Patios 4

Makuhari, Japan
1995

1

communal facilities, commercial spaces and parking. Above this platform is the housing grouped around the courtyard which is private to residents. There are two kinds of housing block, "separate" with two housing units on each floor and "continuous" made up of a series of "thin" housing units - the separate types face the ocean and the sun whilst the continuous helps screen the project from the north wind and forms the main elevation towards the "Promenade". The lofty voids between dwellings help with sunlight penetration and the scheme to communicate with its surroundings.

The courtyard is beautifully landscaped with a variety of plants so that there is something in bloom all year round. Tall trees, precast paviors with surface patterns that convey the image of a beach boardwalk all add to the quality of the space.

Further reading

Spazio e Societa
vol. 18, no. 74, 1996 Apr./June, pp. 74-79
Text in Italian & English

GA Japan: Environmental Design
no. 15, 1995 July-Aug., pp. 126-134
Text in Japanese

Shinkenchiku
1995 Apr., pp. 270-275
Text in Japanese

2

1   Exterior view
2   General view
3   View from promenade

3

4

5

6

4   View of community entrance
5   Northwest elevation
6   View from sea side

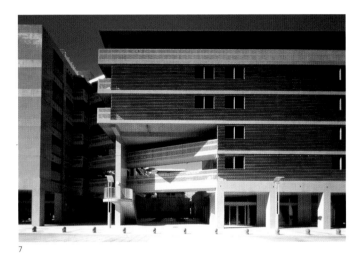

7

8

9

7   Promenade side elevation
8   General view of courtyard
9   View of entrance from promenade

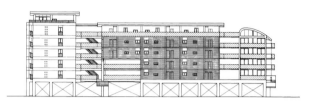

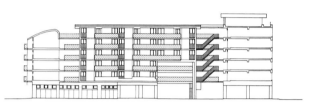

10

1st floor

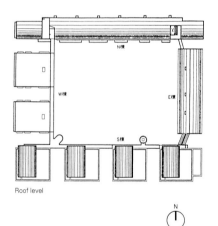

Roof level

N

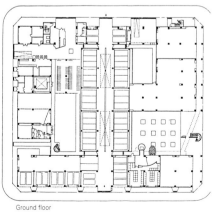

Ground floor

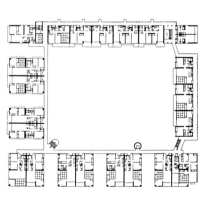

3rd, 4th floor

10   Elevations & sections
11   Plans

11

Narrow Street, on the north bank of the River Thames in Limehouse, is one of London Docklands most historic streets. The whole area has been transformed from former waterfront wharves and warehouses to new residential and commercial development.

Roy Square makes a genuine attempt to create private housing of urban quality taking its inspiration from the architects' close study of the timeless qualities and proportions of the nearby Georgian streets and squares (Figs 5 and 6). The ground floor is taken up with workshops, entrances, stairs and lifts to the dwellings above and the garaging of cars. The housing is grouped around a rectangular court that is entered from a flight of stairs off Narrow Street. The main entrance to all dwellings is from this courtyard. The accommodation is of

Credits & data

Location: Narrow Street, Limehouse,
    London E14, UK
Number of dwellings: 84
Site area: 0.4 ha (1acre)
Density: 210 dwellings/ha (84 dwellings/acre)
Typical dwelling sizes:
    1-bedroom flats: 37-57m^2 (397-613ft^2)
    2-bedroom flats: 61-80m^2 (656-860ft^2)
    3-bedroom flats: 117m^2 (1,258ft^2)
Parking:
    communal garage beneath the project.

1

Ian Ritchie Architects

Roy Square

London, UK
1988

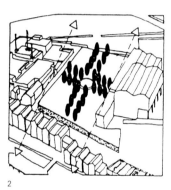
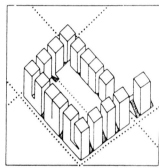

2

very high quality consisting mostly of flats at lower level with maisonettes above. All are lit by large glazed bay windows or conservatories that face the square, or by deep windows opening onto balconies.

The form of the central space and the large bay windows take their cue from the proportioning principles identified in architects' study. The articulation of the terraces into pavilions reflects the rhythm and scale of central London urban houses. On the other hand, the pools at each end of the courtyard linked by a narrow channel and the lush planting gives the court a decidedly Mogul appearance. The water gathers in an oblong basin, runs along the channel set along the centre of the square, then disappears below ground to reappear as a small cascade each side of the entrance staircase.

Further reading

Architects' Journal
vol. 189, no. 6, 1989 Feb. 8, pp. 24-29
Text in English

Baumeister
vol. 88, no. 8, 1991 Aug., pp. 28-31
Text in German

Architecture d'Aujourd'hui
no. 266, 1989 Dec., pp. 114-115
Text in French

1   Exterior view on Narrow Street
2   Concept study

3

3   Looking into the square from the entrance
4   West view on the square

5

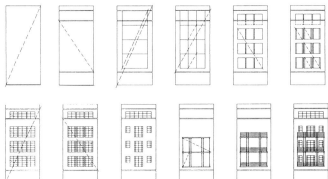

6

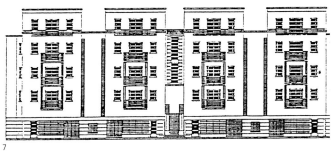

7

8

5   Elevation
6   Elevation study
7   View on Northey Street
8   South view on the square

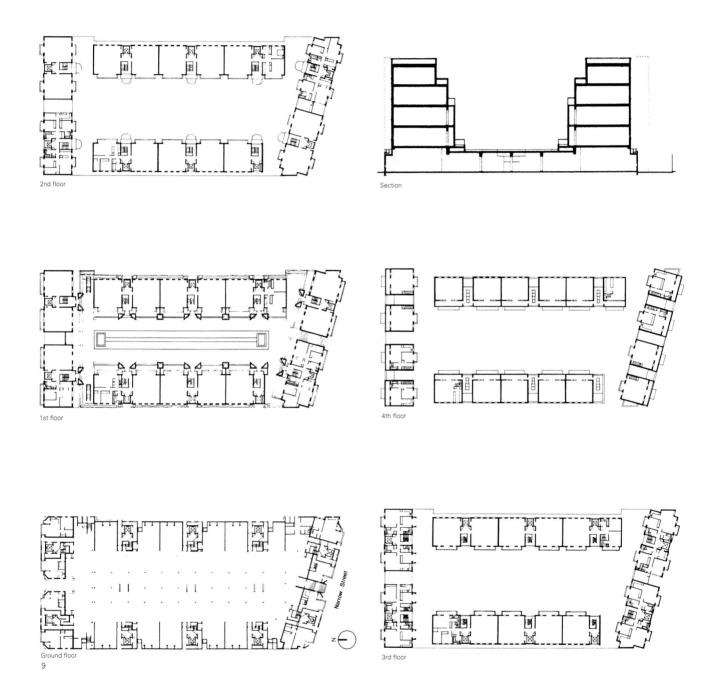

2nd floor

Section

1st floor

4th floor

Ground floor

9

3rd floor

Narrow Street

N

9   Plans and section

Chapter 5
Density: Over 90 Dwellings Per Acre

Murray Grove, built by the Peabody Housing Trust, is a pioneer for the UK in modular construction combined with high levels of prefabrication. Despite being commonplace in countries such as Japan and Scandinavia, where it is possible to purchase a customised home from a catalogue of components, this form of construction has yet to be accepted in Britain. The concept reflects "Rethinking Construction", produced in 1998 by the UK government's Construction Task Force chaired by Sir John Egan [1] which aimed at modernising the construction industry, particularly house building in the social sector. The case for modularisation is speed of construction, quality control through off-site production, and economy provided there is sufficient volume of housing produced.

Credits & data

Location: Murray Grove, Hackney,
    London, UK
Number of dwellings: 24
Site Area: 0.10 ha (0.25 acres)
Density: 240 dwellings/ha (96 dwellings/acre)

Further reading

Architects' Journal
vol. 210, no. 20, 1999 Nov. 25, pp. 25-34
Text in English

World Architecture
no. 86, 2000 May, pp. 88-89
Text in English

Architecture Today
no. 96, 1999 Mar., pp. 60-64
Text in English

Cartwright Pickard

Murray Grove

London, UK
1999

1

The scheme comprises two 5-store wings of flats along Murray Grove and Shepherdess Walk. These enclose a courtyard at the rear, which contains 3 car parking spaces. At the corner, the entrance, lift and staircase form a dramatic tower. Flat entrances, bathrooms and kitchens face the street whilst living and bedrooms overlook the quiet courtyard.

The flats are formed from room modules constructed in the factory as a steel box with internal walls and injected insulation between plasterboard on the inside and galvanised steel sheet on the outside. These represent 50 percent of the total costs. One-bedroom flats are assembled from 2 modules whilst the two-bedroom flats have a third module in the centre to provide the extra bedroom and a larger kitchen. The modules are clad externally with red cedar and terracotta panels. The external

galleries and balconies are constructed by more traditional means although with a high degree of prefabrication.

[1] Construction Task Force, Rethinking Construction (1998), Department of the Environment, Transport and the Regions, UK.

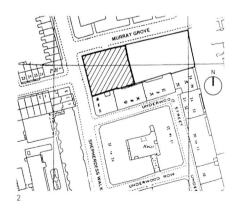

2

1 General exterior view
2 Location plan
3 Night view of street side

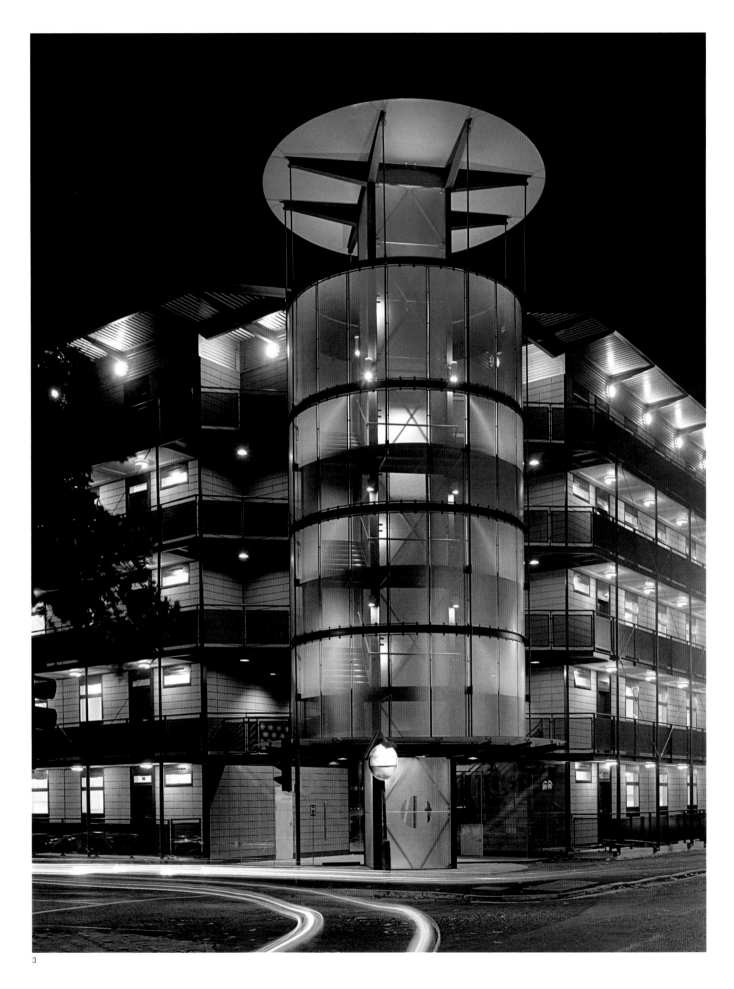

3

4

5

6

4 Façade along the street
5 View on the courtyard
6 View of balconies

7

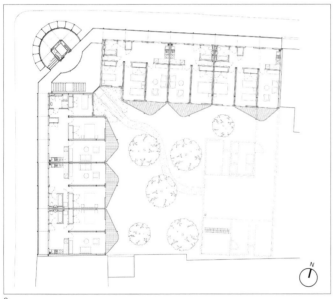

8

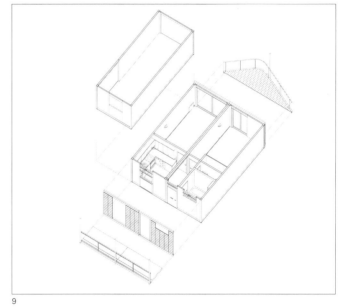

9

10

7   View of living room

8   1st floor plan

9   1-bedroom dwelling

10 View of kitchen

The Bercy housing project by Christian Portzamparc is part of the regeneration of the Bercy quartier of Paris, which extends over 40 hectares and includes the Palais Omnisports stadium and a new urban park. The master plan was developed by Jean-Pierre Buffi who stipulated that a sequence of neo-Hassman "ilots" should be created, each 80 metres long by 20 metres wide (262 x 66 ft.) to form an edge to the urban park. The ilots were to relate to the wider city in terms of height regulation, massing and urban space, mixed use and a clear definition of public and private space.

Six different architectural practices designed six blocks of housing, each of which was built with its own inner courtyard and all the blocks were linked together by south-facing balconies.

Credits & data

Location: 37-45 extension of rue de Pommard,
     Bercy, Paris, France
Number of dwellings: 67
Site area: 0.28 ha (0.69 acres)
Density: 239 dwellings/ha (97 dwellings/acre)
Parking: Underground parking

1

Christian de Portzamparc
Housing on Parc de Bercy
Paris, France
1994

Christian Portzamparc's project is located on the east side of the project. The other architects arranged their blocks to be partly open to the park and closed off from the street. Portzamparc designed an opening on the north side dividing the building into two parts. This opening encourages a conversation between the housing block and the street, and it provides individuality to the scheme making the building different to the others. The two towers located on the south side are quite distinctive. Facing the park are verandas, balconies and greenery conveying natural sunny messages for the residents. The walls are receded for more sunlight, and glazed, vertical and horizontal bay windows let in an abundance of natural light into the rooms. The angles of the walls facing the courtyard lend a good view of it.

Further reading

Architecture d'Aujourd'hui
no. 295, 1994 Oct., pp. 72-79
Text in French. Summaries in English

Techniques et Architecture
no. 412, 1994 Feb.-Mar., pp. 31-42
Text in French

Architectural Review
vol. 184, no. 1180, 1995 Jun., pp. 66-71
Text in English

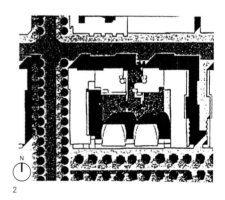

2

1   General exterior view
2   Site plan
3   Exterior view seen from the park

4

4　Wooden passage to the courtyard
5　Entrance view from the street
6　Drawings
　a　Double-light living room
　b　Section
　c　Typical floor plan

5

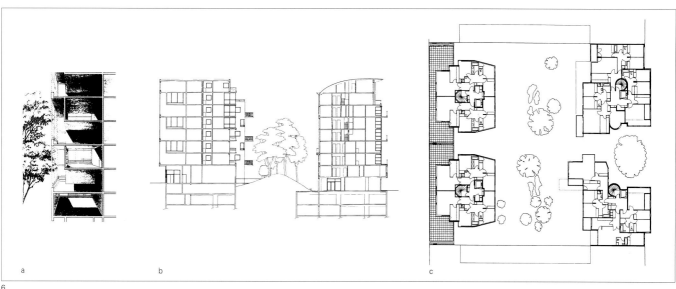

a

b

c

6

Labyrinth is a remarkable housing project developed in the late 1980's. It consists of 22 rental units with various dwelling types ranging from studios to three bedroom apartments.

The housing clusters around the perimeter of the site creating a multi-level courtyard which reflects Kunihiko Hayakawa's long held interest in creating a "semi-public space" that creates a relationship between the private areas of the individual dwellings and their communal territory to the outside roadways, and the wider city, which in this scheme is reflected in allowing people to pass through the development from streets on the north and south sides of the development. In his own description, the architect comments," I remain convinced that apartment buildings in cities must not be worlds closed to all but their residents. Instead, they

Credits & data

Location: 1-26-8 Igusa, Suginami-ku,
    Tokyo, Japan
Number of dwellings: 22
Site area: 0.088 ha (0.22 acres)
Density: 250 dwellings/ha (100 dwellings/acre)
Structure: Reinforced concrete

Kunihiko Hayakawa Architect & Associates
Labyrinth
Tokyo, Japan
1989

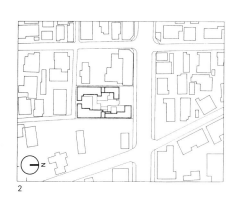
1

must be opened to their urban environments". In Tokyo the principle clearly works but would it be so successful in a western environment?

The apartments are inward looking to the courtyard but the variety of levels and staircases set at various angles gives them a high degree of privacy. At ground floor level they are lifted half a floor above courtyard level. In this way, the project basically possesses a self-contradictory character of being consciously private, yet open to the public domain.

The facades to the courtyard are full of cheerful expression through the use of bright and colourful walls, which are adorned with various geometric openings. All of these features make a vivid and lively environment for the residents, and also for people passing through.

Further reading

Japan Architect
vol. 64, no. 10 (390), 1989 Oct., pp. 35-41
Text in English

SD
no. 304 (1), 1990 Jan., pp. 24-29
Text in Japanese

Nikkei Architecture
1989 July 10, pp. 184-190
Text in Japanese

2

1   View of the west wing from the south-east
2   Site plan
3   Looking down into the courtyard

3

4

4   View of the west wing from the north-east
5   South side façade of the west wing

5

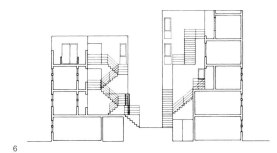

6

7

8

6   Sections
7   View on the courtyard from the south-west
8   View on the courtyard from the north-west

2nd floor

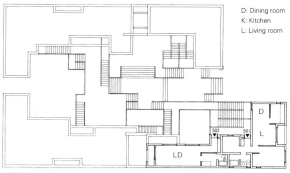

D: Dining room
K: Kitchen
L: Living room

4th floor

1st floor

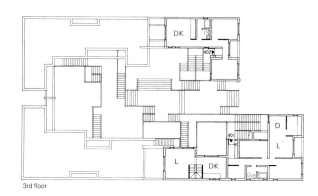

3rd floor

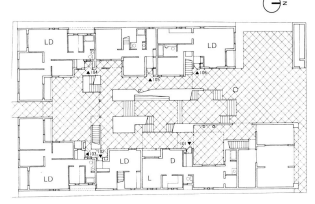

Ground floor

9

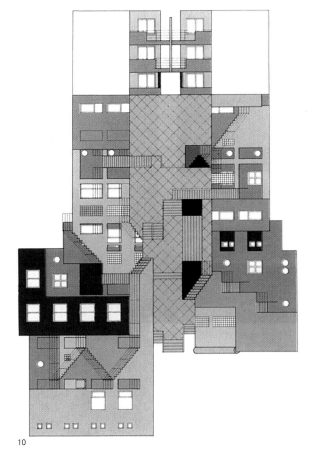

10

9 Plans
10 Elevations, schematic drawing

The project was designed within the planning codes for building height limits, street pattern, space for shops, landscaping, etc., set out at the planning stage of the Makuhari development (see pp. 231-235). It is a fine example of modern Japanese high-density housing.

The architects' concept interrelates two building forms: "silent" heavyweight blocks of housing made of monolithic concrete loadbearing walls and "active" lightweight structures placed strategically within the scheme. The heavyweight blocks, punctured with openings in rhythmic repetition, shape a formed spatial arrangement of housing around garden courtyards. To catch sunlight the walls of these blocks inflect slightly, or they gently bend to accommodate lightweight structures. The "active" lightweight buildings contrast with

Credits & data
Interiors of apartments architects: Koichi Sone
    & Toshio Enomoto of Kajima Design
Location: 2-14 Utase, Mihama-ku,
    Chiba, Japan
Number of dwellings: 190
Site Area: 0.84 ha (2.07 acres)
Density: 226 dwellings/ha (91.5 dwellings/acre)
Number of parking spaces/garages: 195
Structure: reinforced concrete

Steven Holl Architects

Makuhari Bay Town Patios 11

Makuhari, Japan
1996

1

the monumentality of the blocks. They are a celebration of the miniature and of the organic with each of the forms responding to a specific function - East Gate House (Sunlight Reflecting House), North Gate House (Colour Reflecting House), North Court House (Tea House), South Court House/Public Meeting Room (House of Blue Shadow), West Gate House (House of Fallen Persimmon), and South Gate House (Public Observation Deck/House of Nothing).

The arrangement of the dwellings, choice and colour of building materials, semi-secluded gardens that are beautifully planted, and the perspective arrangement of the activist housing form an inner journey within the project. The reflections of the buildings in the pools of water help create a calm serene atmosphere. This is all made possible by placing the car parking mainly underground.

Further reading
Architectural Record
vol. 185, no. 1, 1997 Jan., pp. 64-77
Text in English

Domus
no. 783, 1996 Jun., pp. 10-19
Text in Italian & English

Deutsche Bauzetschrift
vol. 45, no. 11, 1997 Nov., pp. 41-46
Text in German

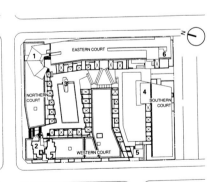

2

1. East Gate Houses / Sunlight Reflecting House
2. North Gate House / Colour Reflecting House
3. North Court House / Tea House
4. South Court House / Public Meeting Room, House of Blue Shadow
5. West Gate House / House of Fallen Persimmon
6. South Gate House / Public Observation Deck, House of Nothing

1   General view of Makuhari Bay Town
2   Site plan

3

4

5

3   Exterior view from the south
4   Exterior view from the east
5   View of West Gate House
    & Western Court along the street
6   View on Western Court

7

8

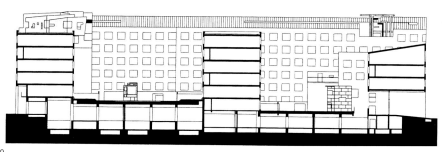

7   View of East Gate from the courtyard
8   South Gate House (the Public Observation Deck)
       on the roof of the eastern building
9   Section

9

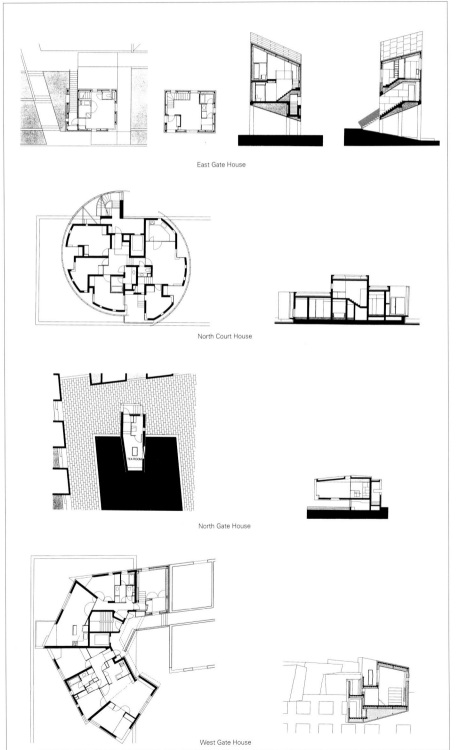

East Gate House

North Court House

North Gate House

TEA ROOM

West Gate House

10

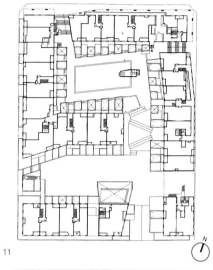

11

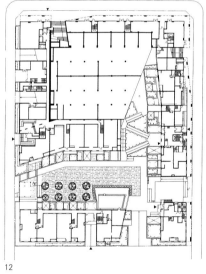

12

10 Houses plan & section
11 1st floor plan
12 Ground floor

Many of the IBA (Internationale Bauausstellung Berlin) housing projects had distinctively individual design themes (see also pp. 100-101). In the case of this project, its originality lies in constructing a "block in block" courtyard form of housing.

The basis of the layout is a central, square courtyard, 20m x 20m (65 x 65ft) in size, with a tree and hard paving. The courtyard is physically enclosed by the four inner walls of the six-storey apartment buildings around it, but access into it is entirely open. On each of the four blocks are two, 3-storey high openings that serve as entrances into the courtyard. These gateways, in turn, divide the complex below the fourth floor into eight independent structures. They also link the project with immediate environment outside the block, its playgrounds, parks and other

Credits & data

Location: Kothener Strasse 35-37,
    Berlin, Germany
Number of dwellings: 43
Dwelling types:
    Flats: 27
    Maisonettes: 16
Site area: 0.16 ha (0.40 acres)
Density: 269 dwellings/ha (108 dwellings/acre)
Typical dwelling sizes:
    54-145m^2 (581-1,561ft^2)
Parking: Underground parking
Structure: Concrete

Oswald Mathias Ungers

Housing on Kothener Strasse

Berlin, Germany
1989

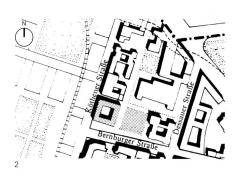

1

facilities. The roof planting and green area in front of the block act as protection along Bernburger Street. Conservatories and anti-noise glazing measure reduce environmental problems.

The scheme includes 27 flats and 16 maisonettes. The courtyard, lifts, staircases (located at the four corners of the courtyard) and the rooftop porch form a network accessible to all households, and they link the block into a single community. Classical symmetry and homogeneity are given a modern interpretation in the design of the four façades of these buildings.

This scheme is an excellent example of how contemporary architectural design can achieve a good quality environment at high density in a limited space in an urban part of a city. It is a brave endeavour and an excellent example to all those looking to design to similar densities.

Further reading

IBA 1987 Project Report
Internationale Bauausstellung Berlin 1987, pp. 100-101
Text in English

A&U
1987 May, extra edition, p. 149
Text in Japanese, captions in English

2

1   Exterior view
2   Location plan

3

3   View seen from the children's playground
4   Axonometric drawing

4

5

6

Section

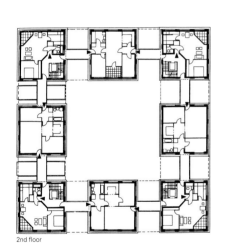

2nd floor

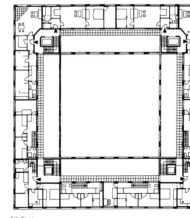

5th floor

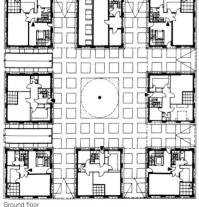

Ground floor

7

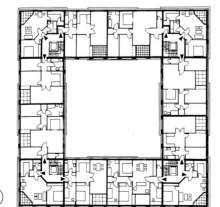

3rd floor

5   Entrance to the courtyard
6   View on the courtyard
7   Plan and section

Renzo Piano's Rue de Meaux Housing is a superb example of simplicity in the design of low cost apartment housing in an urban location. The project represents a very positive attempt to reinvestigate appropriate solutions to the provision of housing in Paris. The design gives a choice of 40 different plan forms arranged in four buildings around a closed-off central garden. The short sides of the rectangle are interrupted by two vertical passageways, dividing the façade into three blocks that continue the scale of the surrounding buildings and maintain the line of shop-fronts along the street. The end buildings extend beyond the width of the garden walls to connect the scheme to adjacent buildings. In places the building recedes as stepped terraces on upper stories.

The 66m x 25m x 25m high (217 x 82 x 82ft.)

Credits & data

Location: 64 Rue de Meaux, 19e,
    Paris, France
Number of dwellings: 220
Other accommodation: 3 shops
Site area: 0.72 ha (1.78 acres)
Density: 306 dwellings/ha (124 dwellings/acre)
Parking: Underground garaging

Renzo Piano Building Workshop

Rue de Meaux Housing

Paris, France
1991

1

central courtyard is the heart of the project. It corresponds in volume to a medium-sized Paris street though its character is very different. The tall slender silver birch trees resemble bamboo and provide visual and aural privacy. The effect is of a peaceful green island in which to escape from the clamour of the outside streets. It is an open-air living room shared by all the residents where they can meet, talk and rest under a canopy of trees.

Equally interesting is the elevational treatment of solids and voids (and slatted voids), glazed and red terracotta tile hanging. To provide security, dwellings have aluminium louvred blinds outside the glazing, which can be opened and closed at will by the residents. Shutters or fabric blinds have been provided elsewhere which add an extra dimension to visual variety.

Further reading
Architectural Review
vol. 190, no. 1141, 1992 Mar., pp. 35-40
Text in English

Domus
no. 729, 1991 July-Aug., pp. 29-39
Text in Italian and English

A&U
no. 3, 1989 Mar. extra edition, pp. 240-241
Text in English & Japanese

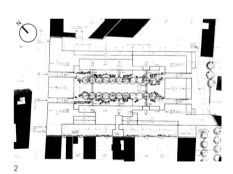

2

1   View on courtyard
2   Site plan

3

4

5

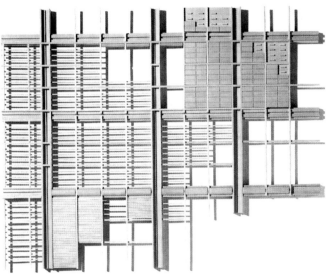

6

7

8

5   Façade along the street

6,7&8   Details of façade

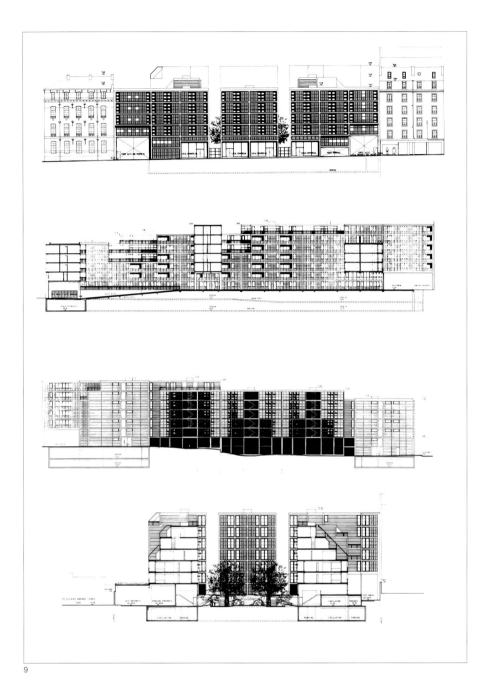

9

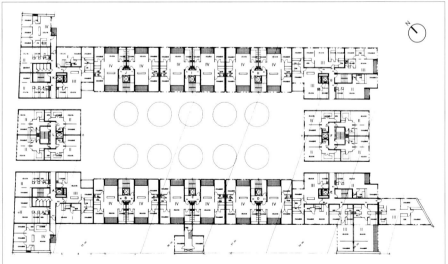

10

9 Elevations & sections
10 Typical floor plan

Borneo Sporenburg

Borneo-Sporenburg is a former harbour area along the shore of the Het IJ near Amsterdam's inner city. The 17,000 dwelling redevelopment plan was intended to resemble Jordaan, Amsterdam's lively inner-city quarter. The City Council therefore set up a condition for a minimum overall density of 100 dwellings per hectare (40 dwellings per acre). 30% of the dwellings were to be subsidised social housing.

The developers requested the municipality agree a "suburban" form, which was reflected in low-rise, single family town houses, given rhythm by the variation of blocks and open spaces. This was given an urban feel through a 3.5m (11.ft 6ins) high ground floor to allow for both living and working. Double height spaces were specified for canal-side units to draw light inside. Some areas

Credits & data
Master Plan of Borneo-Sporonburg:
  Adrian, Geuze, West 8, Rotterdam
Location: Borneo-Sporonburg 9,
  Amsterdam, the Netherlands
Number of dwellings: 214
Other accommodation: 1,100m^2(11,825ft^2) business space
Site area: 0.5 ha (1.3 acres)
Density: 428 dwellings/ha (173 dwellings/acre)
Number of parking spaces: 179

Further Reading
A&U
no. 5(380), 2002 May, pp. 62-67
Text in English & Japanese

Domus
no. 839, 2001 July/Aug., pp. 128-143
Text in Italian & English

World Architecture
no. 93, 2001 Feb., pp. 64-67
Text in English

de Architekten Cie. Amsterdam, Frits van Dongen

The Whale

Amsterdam, The Netherlands
2000

1

were designated for individual houses, each designed by the buyers' own architect and given a different canal side appearance.

The development includes a school, small park and three graceful pedestrian bridges that arch over the waterways. A diagonal pattern, cut through the grid of townhouses focuses on nearby landmarks such as the spired central train station and a monumental pumping station.

The Whale

Within the Borneo Sporenburg development, there are three skewed "meteorite" buildings. The Master Plan stipulated that these be larger, courtyard style apartment buildings to serve a picturesque visual function as cathedrals and churches of historic towns. The Whale has a similar footprint as a "Berlage block"- 100 x 50m (328ft x 164ft) - in Amsterdam-Zuid but it contains twice

the accommodation. By elevating the building on two sides the lower floors receive sunlight coming in from under the actual building, which ensures light enters into the heart of the project. Business units are located on the ground floor and there is a large underground car park.

From its conservatories the Whale offers a wide view of Amsterdam's inner city and across the expansive waters of the Het IJ. It exudes an atmosphere of intimacy through the wood finishing and the inner garden. The diagonal lines are reproduced in the interior of the building in a staggered pattern of galleries. These give access both to the dwellings on the shared level and to those on the floor above. Each of the elevated corners is supported by a glass stairway with a lift. On the outside, the taut lines are continued in the aluminium roof and the zinc frontage material.

1 Aerial view of Borneo-Sporonburg
2 Aerial view of the Whale

2

3

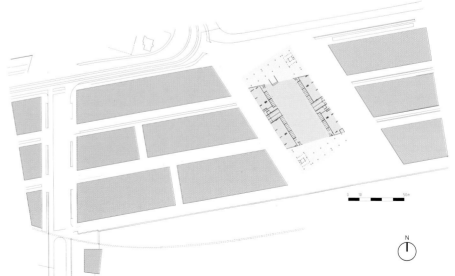

3   Exterior night view
4   Site plan
5   Night view of the courtyard garden

4

5

6

7

8

6   View of façade of courtyard side
7   Access corridor
8   View of ground level

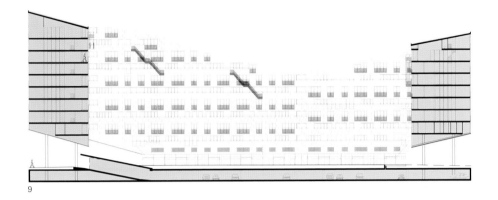

9

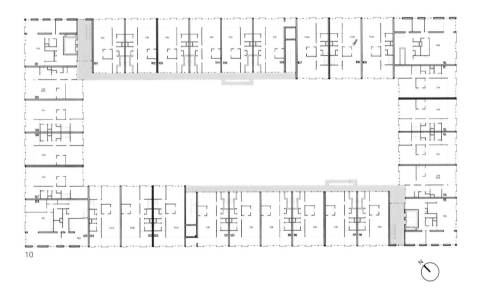

10

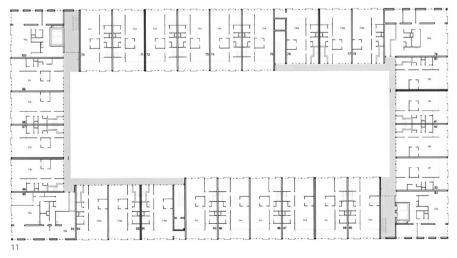

11

9   Elevation
10   5th floor plan
11   4th floor plan

Index - by architect

Bibliography

Atelier 5

Werk, Bauen & Wohnen, vol. 78/45, no. 6, 1991 June, pp. 34-38

Werk, Bauen & Wohnen, no. 5, 1994 May, pp. 1-6, after p. 94

Architecture Today, no. 51, 1994 Sept., pp. 14-15

Chapman Taylor Partners

Building, Housing Project Design Awards 1991, vol. 256, no. 7721 (46)
    supplement, 1991 Nov. 15, pp. 20-21

Charles Cooper + Harrison Ince

Building, vol. 266, no. 8168 (2), 2001 Jan. 12, pp. 40-45

Corrigan + Soundy + Kilaiditi

Building, vol. 253, no. 24, 1988 Jun, pp. 41-48

CZWG Architects

Architectural Review, vol. 204, no. 1222, 1998 Dec., pp. 54-57

RIBA Book of 20th Century British Housing, Colquhoun, I.,
    Architectural Press/Butterworth Heinemann, 1999, pp. 135-136

Building, 1997 Nov., Brick Awards, p. 52

David Killroy Architects

A&U, no. 7(298), 1995 July, pp. 98-109

Progressive Architecture, vol. 75, no. 5, 1994 May, pp. 49-55

Architectural Review, vol. 193, no. 1161, 1993 Nov., pp. 56-57

Gunther Domenig

Housing Design: An International Perspective
    Colquhoun, I., and Fauset, P. G., B. T. Batsford, 1991, pp. 220-222

Architectural Review, vol. 184, no. 1102, 1988 Dec., pp. 73-75

Deutsche Bauzeitschrift,, vol. 39, no. 4, 1991 Apr., pp. 495-502

Frits van Dongen

A&U, no. 5(380), 2002 May, pp. 62-67

Domus, no. 839, 2001 July/Aug., pp. 128-143

World Architecture, no. 93, 2001 Feb., pp. 64-67

Takao Endo

Nikkei Architecture, no. 21, 1991 Jan., pp. 69-76

Kunihiko Hayakawa

GA Houses, no. 38, 1993 July, pp. 150-165

Japan Architect, 1994 spring, no. 13, pp. 200-203

SD, no. 304 (1), 1990 Jan., pp. 24-29

Herman Hertzberger

Architectural Review, vol. 182, no. 1085, 1987 July, pp. 63-65

GA Houses, no. 23, 1988 Aug., pp. 120-127

de Architect, 1998 Mar., pp. 72-77

Steven Holl

Architectural Record, vol. 185, no. 1, 1997 Jan., pp. 64-77

Domus, no. 783, 1996 Jun,, pp. 10-19

Ian Ritchie Architects

Architects' Journal, vol. 189, no. 6, 1989 Feb. 8, pp. 24-29

Baumeister, vol. 88, no. 8, 1991 Aug., pp. 28-31

Architecture d'Aujourd'hui, no. 266, 1989 Dec., pp. 114-115

Inken & Hinrich Baller

Aktuelles Bauen, vol. 19, no. 11, 1984 Nov, pp. 24-27

GA Houses, no. 23, 1988 Aug., pp. 136-143

Kohsuke Izumi

Nikkei Architecture, no. 21, 1991 Jan., pp. 113-124

Jestico & Whiles

Architects' Journal, vol. 199, no. 10, 1994 Mar. 9, pp. 45-55

Building, vol. 260, no. 7914 (43) supplement, 1995 Oct. 27, p. 23

Merih Karaaslan

SD, no. 7(346), 1993 July, pp. 14-15

Rolf Keller

Architectural Review, vol. 177, no. 1060, 1985 June, pp. 66-75

Detail, vol. 24, no. 6, 1984 Nov.-Dec., pp. 675-676

Kojiro Kitayama

Nikkei Architecture, 1992 July 6, pp. 202-207

Zyuutaku Tokusyuu, 1992 Aug., pp. 115-127

Yasumitsu Matsunaga

Kenchiku Bunka, 1990 Jun., vol.45, no. 524, pp. 165-175

Zyuutaku Tokusyuu, 1990 Jun., pp. 124-132

Shinkenchiku, 1995 Apr., pp. 270-275

GA Japan, no. 1, 1999 May, pp. 134-141

Georges Maurios

Architectural Review, vol. 188, no. 1124, 1990 Oct., pp. 76-80

Mills Beaumont Leavey

Building, vol. 261, no. 7945, 1996 Sept. 6, pp. 38-43

Architects' Journal, vol. 205, no. 13, 1997 Apr. 3, p. 34

Moore Ruble Yudell Architects & Planners

Landscape Architecture, vol. 83, no. 7, 1993 July, p. 29

Shinkenchiku, 1992 May., pp. 247-256

Design Out Crime, Colquhoun, I., Architectural Press, 2004, pp. 253-255

Architectural Record, vol. 190, no. 2, 2002 Feb., pp. 156-158

Abitare, no. 409, 2001 Sept., pp. 74-78

Oswald Mathias Ungers

IBA 1987 Project Report,
    Internationale Bauausstellung Berlin 1987, pp. 100-101

A&U, 1987 May, extra edition; p. 149

Renzo Piano

Architectural Review , vol. 190, no. 1141, 1992 Mar., pp. 35-40

Domus, no. 729, 1991 July-Aug., pp. 29-39

A&U, no. 3, 1989 Mar. extra edition, pp. 240-241

Cartwright Pickard

Architects' Journal, vol. 210, no. 20, 1999 Nov. 25, pp. 25-34

Christian de Portzamparc

Architecture d'Aujourd'hui, no. 295, 1994 Oct., pp. 72-79

Techniques et Architecture, no. 412, 1994 Feb.-Mar., pp. 31-42

Abitare, no. 192, 1981 Mar, pp. 64-69

Raj Rewal

Architectural Review, vol. 201, no. 1204, 1997 Jun., pp. 58-61

Korean Architects, 1995 Oct., pp. 58-60

Sandy & Babcock International

Urban Land , vol. 51, no. 8, 1992 Aug, pp. 40-41

Alain Sarfati

Architects' Journal, 1984 Jan. 25, pp. 46-55

Domus, 1982 July, pp. 12-13

Mario Schjetnan

World Collective Houses: 200 in the 20th century
Yoshinobu Ashihara, Daikyo 30th Anniversary Publication,
    Japan, 1990, p. 297

Anton Schweighofer

Casabella, vol. 51, no. 540, 1987 Nov., pp. 38-41

Werk, Bauen & Wohnen, vol. 76/43, no. 5, 1989 May, pp. 40-49

Szyszkowitz - Kowalski

Architectural Review, no. 1161, 1993 Nov., pp. 40-44

GA Houses, no. 43, 1994 Oct., pp. 148-151

GA Houses, no. 41, 1994 Mar., pp. 144-152

Architectural Review, vol. 206, no. 1233, 1999 Nov., pp. 47-51

Heinz Tesar

Bauforum, vol. 18, no. 111, 1985, pp. 51-57

Skala, no. 5, 1986 Aug., p. 7

Domus, no. 672, 1986 May, pp. 1-3

Tegnestuen Vandkunsten

Arkitektur DK , vol. 36, no. 1-2, 1992, pp. 16-19

Guide To Danish Architecture 2, Kim Dirchinck-Holmfeld,
    Arkitektens Forlag, 1995, p. 214

Liyangyong Wu

Architectural Review , vol. 207, no. 1236, 2000 Feb, pp. 73-75

Architectural Journal, no. 2, 1991 Feb., pp. 7-13

Photograph Credits

In addition to Liyang Sun's photographs and those I took myself, architects and photographers provided photographs as follows:

Ian Colquhoun for 15-21/all; 76/5; 178/4; 181-184/1,3,5,6,8
Gunter Hauer for 25/1; 69-72/1,3,4,7
Anna Blau for 26-27/3,4
Szyszkowitz-Kowalski for 28/5,6
Raj Rewal for 30-34/1,3,5-8
David Killory Architects for 35-38/1,3,4,7,8
Mario Schjetnan, Jorge Sandoval for 40-44/1-7
Koji Horiuchi for 45-49/1,3-6,9-11; 145-149/1,3,5-8; 205-207/3-9
H. Tesar for 55-56/1,3
Herman Hertzberger for 65-68/1,3-5
Jay Graham for 78-82/1,3-6
Merih Karaaslan for 87-90/1,3-8
Moore Ruble Yudell for 113-117/1,3,5,7-10; 177-180/1,3,7,8,11
James Mary O'Connor for 179/5,6
Liyangyong Wu for 122-124/1-5
Daria Scagliola & Stijn Brakkee for 126-130/1,3-6,8,9
Deidi von Schaewen for 131-134/1,3-6,9
Jo Reid & John Peck for 140-144/1,2,6
Uwe Rau for 153-157/1,3-6
Zhonggu Wang for 189-192/1-7
Jeroen Musch for 199-202/1,3-6,8; 244-249/1-3,5-8
Cartwright Pickard Architects & Yorkon for 217-221/1,3-7,10

Jingmin Zhou, BEng, MEng, PhD in Architecture.
A specialist researcher in the area of living environment.
She has spent a number of years doing research in Britain, Japan and Canada
and has published two books on housing design.